ALSO BY LISA KRÖGER AND
MELANIE R. ANDERSON

*Monster, She Wrote: The Women Who
Pioneered Horror and Speculative Fiction*

Toil & Trouble

A WOMEN'S HISTORY
OF THE OCCULT

Lisa Kröger and
Melanie R. Anderson

QUIRK BOOKS
PHILADELPHIA

Full Library of Congress Cataloging-in-Publication Data
available upon request.

ISBN: 978-1-68369-291-1

Printed in Singapore
Typeset in Bagolen, GT Haptik, Maiola, and Degular
Designed by Elissa Flanigan
Production management by John J. McGurk

Quirk Books
215 Church Street
Philadelphia, PA 19106
quirkbooks.com

10 9 8 7 6 5 4 3 2 1

FOR EVERYONE WHO
DARES TO BE 100%
THAT WITCH

CONTENTS

INTRODUCTION

n July 2020, at a time when we arguably did not need more problems, a group of young witches tried to hex the moon.

It doesn't really matter why, or whether they were successful (the moon's still here, so maybe not). In fact, it's not clear how many people were involved or how serious they were; people outside the online occult community found out about the event through social media posts about what the so-called baby witches were planning and why it was a bad idea, and through a cascade of news stories about the rumor on sites like BuzzFeed. That doesn't really matter either. What's important is that there's an online occult community at all—and not only that, but a community so robust and popular that it is able to sustain fringe groups (like the witches who hexed the moon) and warring factions (like the people who suggested that maybe they shouldn't). What's also important is that all of this happened in public.

This would have been unthinkable to women in seventeenth-century New England—even if they could get past the idea of the internet. *Witch* used to be an accusation with potentially fatal consequences, not an identity to proudly display (and endlessly debate) in the public square. Those long-ago women might be similarly shocked by the recent popularity of crystals, tarot cards, and astrology memes. "In an age of uncertainty, dislocation and environmental turmoil, younger generations are taking a renewed interest in astrology, horoscopes, and the occult," wrote Josh Walker in a 2020 *Wired* article.

That "renewed interest" is more like a tidal wave. On the social video app TikTok, which is popular with people in their teens and twenties, the hashtag #witchtok garnered more than two billion views in 2019 and 2020. Driving those views were videos offering everything from good-luck spells to protection potions—in other words, predictability in times of uncertainty. After all, young adults in 2020 were getting ready to enter the world in scary times: economic downturn, a terrible job market, political uncertainty, public protests, and a pandemic raging out of control.

But it's more than just difficult times that are responsible for young people's—especially young women's—interest in the occult. From the start of the United States, whose colonial period coincided with the violent witch hunts in Europe of the sixteenth and seventeenth centuries, women have had a close relationship with the occult—at times, whether they wanted one or not. Over the years, women have been variously cast as unnatural, supernatural, angelic, demonic, attuned to death, or in league with the Devil.

So how did we get from Salem to today's proud witches? Centuries of women responded to these accusations by using the occult as a route to power.

When we started working on this book, we wanted to investigate all the ways women interacted with and used occult tools to achieve empowerment. We published our first book, *Monster, She Wrote*, in the fall of 2019. As we started thinking about our next project, we began exploring the ways women's history and the history of the occult intersected. Specifically, we were interested in examining women's occult history in the United States. While we were having these conversations in 2020, our focus kept being pulled toward world events. We won't go into everything here—we all lived through it—but what was fascinating to us was how much the occult was a constant presence. Women everywhere, it seemed, were responding to the pandemic and to the political upheaval of the impending election with what appeared to be a "witchy" attitude. Women on TikTok were explaining how to hex Trump (something that, we learned, witches had been doing since his election in 2016). Witches on Instagram were posting moody "cottagecore" pictures with instructions on how to use herbs to create a spell jar. Mediums on YouTube were gaining large audiences as we all went into quarantine, entertaining us with tarot readings. Astrology apps on phones rose in popularity. Something was happening—but what?

We didn't come to this question as practitioners of the occult. Other than the occasional flip through a tarot deck or attempt to summon a ghostly friend with a Ouija board at a party, we do not participate in any tradition that would fit within the scope of this book. But that doesn't mean that we are dismissive of these traditions; indeed, as academics we appreciate the long, rich history of occult practice, especially its place in women's history.

With this in mind, we do want to offer a word of warning. Unfortunately, this history includes all the problems of American history. At times, the women in these pages were guilty of cultural appropriation. Some used language, particularly during second-wave feminism, that is exclusionary or even insulting toward women who were assigned male at birth. For example, some of the women who worked to bring about the feminist Goddess movement used a lot of womb imagery and phrasing, which, while revolutionary at the time, excludes women who don't have a uterus. Sometimes this exclusion comes from carelessness or ignorance; other times it represents deliberate gatekeeping about who's allowed to be a woman and a witch. We want to be clear here that we do not endorse this kind of language. We support all women, and trans women are women. (Some of the people we've profiled are outside the gender binary; they're here because they're part of the opposition to a male-dominated culture.) We have also highlighted some people who unscrupulously used the occult (and sometimes the fear of the occult) for personal gain, often to the detriment of others. We hope that we handle these moments in this history with care and sensitivity. This history can be seen as an evolution of ideas about what the occult was and could be. In order to understand the whole picture and how we got to the twenty-first century, we've included the various perspectives and debates that drove that progression.

Ultimately, through all these debates and struggles, we see how women use the occult as a positive force, as a way for the disenfranchised to gain more agency in society. Today, we also see people in the occult world having more conversations about inclusivity and equity. The occult pushes barriers and boundaries, and as such, it is always evolving. In this book, every person mentioned is a part of this larger arc toward equity (even if they didn't intend to be), but that doesn't mean that there aren't real problems and issues that need to be called out.

In the end, the stories we uncovered in our research of women and the occult are fascinating, which brings us back to our original thesis. When researching, we asked ourselves a few questions. What constitutes the occult? How does the occult help women, especially when accusations of the occult often end in banishment or, worse, death? If it is a positive thing, then why does it seem that there is a backlash to the occult, or a moral panic, that seems to pop up every few decades?

Women have routinely been drawn to this tradition, in part because US society, with its Christian roots, has always placed the white male at the top of the patriarchal structure. In a way, women have always existed in occulted space. They were meant to be hidden; their role was one that existed behind the scenes, as caretaker of the family and keeper of the home. Their role was never intended to outside of the mainstream to create new traditions and new language, and with them, a new path forward to reclaim some of the power that was taken away. Sometimes those working within the occult were using mainstream ideas to effect change. A good example would be the Spiritualist movement, especially Black Spiritual churches, which used Christian language and frameworks. Of course, that knife cut both ways. The occult was often dismissed, even scrutinized, as the antithesis to conservative and Christian values. We've tried to examine the broad strokes of this occult arc.

In this book, you'll meet some of the women who helped create or design occult systems and symbols, like the artist behind the most iconic tarot deck and the woman who gave the Ouija board its name—and you'll also meet women who became professional skeptics or debunkers to hold people accountable, an important role in keeping the occult world ethical. You'll be introduced to women who used the occult as a stepping-stone to political power, like First Lady Nancy Reagan's personal psychic, and some who used it to find financial security. And you'll get to know a wide array of women who have embraced labels like *witch*, *voodoo queen*, and *Mistress of the Dark*.

The occult in US history takes many forms: from accusations of witchcraft in seventeenth-century New England to the development of Spiritualism in the nineteenth century, to the uses of astrology and fortune-telling in the early twentieth century, to the Goddess movement of the mid-twentieth century, to the Satanic Panic of the 1980s and '90s, and to our current obsessions with psychics, occult paraphernalia, spells, and crystals. Throughout these tumultuous centuries, women have been connected to the occult by the patriarchy as a way of punishing and policing their behavior (for example, the colonial accusations of witchcraft and satanic revels), and women have grasped the occult as an opening to seize independence and power (for example, how the Spiritualist movement gave women voices to speak out about political issues).

As we began thinking about women's relationships with the occult and the power and backlash that can result, we realized that, while we have read a lot of supernatural fiction by women, we've never before delved into all the ways women have participated in the occult and been perceived by the larger society for that participation. What follows are the figures we learned about, the larger social and political issues we pondered, and the stories we want to share about how women, primarily in the United States, have related to their political and social environments through the occult. This relationship seems to ebb and flow over the centuries between cultural backlash and a search for empowerment. It's a vast and complicated history with many twists and turns, but we are excited to lead you on this journey through the occult as it appears in American women's lives, embodied by some of the extraordinary individuals who have designed, politicized, promoted, investigated, and embraced it.

A NOTE ON TERMINOLOGY

I n this book, we'll talk about witchcraft, and also about the occult generally. It's important to note that *the occult* and *witchcraft* are not interchangeable. We will discuss witches, of course, because the history of women's occult involvement is entwined with the history of the witch in the US. But we will also look at how that label is misapplied—sometimes as an insult with real-world harmful consequences, and sometimes as a result of sheer willful ignorance. We do not want to falsely equate witchcraft with the occult generally. However, in our investigative journey, we have found that the two are inextricably linked. When women engage in rebellion in the form of occult resistance, they are labeled witches, for good or for bad.

Today, the word *witch* evokes images of powerful women. Women (and people of all genders) from all walks of life are happy to proudly, loudly proclaim that they are witches. For some, this is a rejection of mainstream organized religion in favor of spiritual practices that are more fluidly defined and that offer acceptance for marginalized identities that have traditionally been shunned or silenced. For others, it is the celebration of a practice passed down from generation to generation, a familial and cultural tradition that once had to be hidden out of fear. It can be a slippery term. When someone calls themselves a witch, that word usually holds an entire world: a history of teachings, a breadth of hard-earned beliefs, and sometimes a very specific tradition from which that witch is building. However, in nonmagic communities, the label is thrown around with little regard to the full bloom of meaning behind it. Anything occult is labeled as witchcraft, and anyone practicing the occult is a witch; in this case, the term is meant to place the person outside the mainstream. What could be a label of power and resistance instead becomes a means of insult and exclusion.

Maybe even more difficult to define is the word *occult*. At its most basic, it simply means something hidden from view. For our use, it's referring to those traditions relating to spiritual and sometimes religious beliefs that have been hidden from mainstream view. The occult world in the United States is broad. It encompasses everything from people who can read auras and energies, working from their homes or streetside setups in places like New Orleans's Jackson Square, to fully incorporated societies whose main mission is to make contact with the spirit world that exists beyond our own.

As we use it in this book, *the occult* refers to a belief in an unknown world that will open the door to hidden knowledge, knowledge that will make the world a better (and often more equal) place. The occult at times intertwines with religion (like Christian mysticism or the Jewish tradition of Kabbalah) and sometimes situates itself in an older tradition (like Goddess worship). At other times, it explodes definitions and situates itself opposed to the mainstream religious beliefs (like the way modern-day Satanism co-opts the Christian image of Satan to tweak the religious right wing). However it is expressed, the occult is meant to bring that hidden knowledge to light.

1

DESIGNING WITCHES

SHAPING THE OCCULT

I s it possible we are living in the golden age of the occult? After all, the occult is all around us today. Suburban housewives regularly burn sage to cleanse their homes. Gentrified neighborhoods have Starbucks on one corner and crystal shops on the next. Tarot cards are sold in Barnes and Noble.

In the past, the word *witch* was used as an insult, an accusation. Those who practiced kept their craft undercover, in the protection of covens, keeping any occult practices secretive. Today, if you casually mention a full moon magical ritual to a neighbor, the worst you'll probably face is a funny look—and you might even make a friend.

But who led us down that path to occult acceptance? How did we get from the Salem witch trials, when any association with the occult could mean a death sentence, to a book like this one, examining women's history with the occult? The evolution was slow and involved many founding mothers taking small steps along the way. These women were at the forefront of a quiet revolution. Their ideas, their words, and their artistry changed the lenses through which Americans viewed religion and spirituality.

America's occult history begins in seventeenth-century Salem, in a new colony that was supposedly built upon the freedom of religion, assuming that religion was Puritan and patriarchal. Anything else was the work of the Devil. Women's rule was relegated to the home, but public power (in the form of money, property, or governing rights) was strictly held by white men. Property was owned by brothers and fathers and then given as a dowry for marriage, transferred to husbands. Women who inherited property who lacked a close male relative to protect them were often taken to court. If legal measures failed to strip a woman of her property, a witch accusation could do the trick. And once you'd disenfranchised a woman by labeling her a witch, you could often hang on to her property for generations. Witchcraft was an insult that could be passed down to daughters and granddaughters, as witchcraft was considered hereditary in those dark early days.

At that time, association with the occult was used to police people's prescribed positions within society, whether religious, political, or economic—and women were frequent targets. Calling a woman a witch was a way to punish her for any behavior that could be interpreted as outside a woman's place in a Puritan community. Whether women were seen as too seductive or too outspoken, the accusation of witchcraft was a warning of what would happen should that power ever be too real. It didn't matter if the occult power was invented; simply the suggestion of it was enough.

Fear of the occult was a way to ensure conformity to society's standards. If a person didn't fit in, then they were labeled as a witch and banished from society—or worse. But something fascinating was brewing here, even as early as Salem in the 1600s. If the occult was a tool used to keep people in line with society, then there would be those who would learn to use that tool for their own benefit. The occult, after all, is nonconformist by its very nature. If people could use the occult as shorthand for invented power to be taken away, then why couldn't women use it as a way to gain power for themselves? What is truly remarkable is that each and every one of these women felt shut out of their own culture. They felt that their ideas weren't represented in their society at large. So they worked to change the very fabric of society, sometimes by working within the system and sometimes by dismantling it completely.

In this chapter, you'll see a few of the women who worked to bring occult ideas and tools into the mainstream. First, there's the Public Universal Friend, a prophet who tried to deconstruct their culture's ideas of gender. In the nineteenth century, the Fox sisters stepped onto the stage and introduced the world to Spiritualism. This movement provided women with career options and, for a few women, even fame. When women ran séances in their homes, they were able to merge their domestic positions with the outside world. More importantly, they had a public forum to voice their political concerns, setting the stage for the later convergence of the occult and second-wave feminism. Following in their footsteps, women like Pamela Colman Smith and Helen Peters Nosworthy designed occult tools still in use today, like the Ouija board and tarot cards. And then there were women in the 1960s and '70s like Starhawk and Z Budapest who designed a female-centered idea of religion that persists to this day.

It's a pattern you'll see repeating in this book: even when they're shut out of controlling or profiting from an industry, organization, or idea, women are often the muscle behind its creation. The figures in this chapter found power through devising, designing, and guiding the occult.

The Public Universal Friend

A SPIRIT GREATER THAN GENDER

I n the mid-nineteenth century, the Spiritualist movement would turn thousands of women into (supposed) conduits for the dead. (We'll hear more about that later when we visit the Fox sisters.) Around seventy years earlier, however, there had already been a shift in spirituality piloted by an individual who had been considered a woman until her early twenties. Unlike the Spiritualist movement to come, this movement's relation to gender was more radical. In 1776, during the tumultuous years of the American Revolution, an often violent time of protest and confusion as colonists tried to define their desires for or fears of creating a new nation, a new religious sect came on the scene: the Society of Universal Friends.

Jemima Wilkinson was born into a large Quaker family in Rhode Island in 1752. Her religion was important to her, and she attended meetings regularly, but she was curious about other denominations, in particular the New Light Baptists, whose revivals she would visit. This period was not only the run-up to the American Revolution, but it was also the time of the Great Awakening, a momentous religious movement, largely spread through revivals. This awakening emphasized a personal salvation experience for believers that involved emotion rather than church and scriptural dogma. Because of Wilkinson's interest in this new movement, in 1776 she was expelled from her Quaker meetings.

After her expulsion, she fell seriously ill. She, her family, and her doctor thought she would die from her extreme fever. Instead, Wilkinson stood up from the bed, declared that Jemima Wilkinson had died and was no more on this Earth, and introduced the people in the room to a new individual: the Public Universal Friend. The Friend explained that the body of Wilkinson had been reanimated to serve as a vessel for a prophet from God. This idea of prophecy wasn't quite like the mediums of the nineteenth century, who would claim to transmit messages from the dead, but it was similar—here, too, a supernatural entity was said to use a human body as a host.

The Public Universal Friend had a couple of messages. First, the Friend was neither female nor male. And second, Christ's return and the end of the world as they knew it were imminent.

The Friend then began preaching their new interpretation of Christianity that incorporated aspects of the Quaker and Baptist faiths in Rhode Island, then in Philadelphia, and finally in the "wilderness" of western New York. The Friend, though, offered more to their followers than other faiths might have been ready for at the time.

The Friend preached the universal personal salvation experience, but included spiritual empowerment as well. In their view, any person could participate in the process of salvation, but unlike in other religions, anyone could also witness and share their faith, regardless of gender or religious training. And this salvation and empowerment were available to male and female acolytes alike. Women were recruited to the faith, known as the Society of Universal Friends, and trained to work in leadership roles as preachers and prophets like the Friend—a practice that was definitely frowned upon by traditional religious groups, which did not allow women to publicly preach. The Friend also strongly advised their followers to be celibate. The women who joined the Society of Universal Friends could use celibacy as a way to access other options for their lives than the socially encouraged roles of wives and mothers.

During the late 1770s and the 1780s, the Society's membership grew. The group attracted members from all classes, including the wealthy and influential. As the group grew and, in particular, after it moved to Philadelphia in 1782, the Friend's insistence on their gender nonconformity was seized upon by critics. The Friend avoided pronouns, whereas their followers used the pronouns *he* and *him* to show the miraculous change the Friend had manifested. (We're using *they* because of the Friend's identity as neither female nor male, even though at the time, *they* and *them* were not generally used as singular gender-neutral pronouns.) The Friend also mixed traditionally feminine and masculine clothes, hairstyles, and behaviors. Historians Tricia L. Noel and Paul B. Moyer noted in a *Throughline* podcast episode for NPR that opponents of the Society tended to use the pronouns *she* and *her* for the Friend, to openly question the Friend's gender representation, and to use the name Jemima Wilkinson when referring to them, thus denying the Friend's chosen identity and spiritual transformation.

The Friend's ahead-of-their-time ideas did not always make them or the Society popular. At one point, a rioting mob attacked the house where the Friend was staying, throwing bricks and invective. After this, in the late 1780s, the Society moved to western New York to what is now Yates County. But the group began to disintegrate. The isolation of their new settlement led to hunger, illness, and a lack of potential converts. Factions formed. The idea of celibacy led to a lack of future generations to carry on the work. The

Friend faced many challenges, but a legal one was the most damaging to their mission. Because the Friend refused to use their legal name of Jemima Wilkinson to sign the deeds of the Society's land, the wealthy men who owned the parcels simply took them from the organization. The Friend had no legal standing in court. Finally, in 1819, the Friend died after struggling with a severe illness, and this time, there was no resurrection.

The Fox Sisters

THE FIRST CELEBRITY SPIRIT MEDIUMS

n late March 1848 (the eve of April Fools' Day, some like to point out), fourteen-year-old Margaretta "Maggie" Fox and her eleven-year-old sister, Catherine, called Kate, were huddled in their bedroom in their family's rented home in Hydesville, New York. The girls had been hearing strange knocks on the walls, which they said were spirits. Through these knocks, they were able to communicate with the ghosts in their home. At first, the system was simple: three knocks for "yes." As the communications continued for the next few days, though, the system grew more complex. They asked the spirits to count, as a way of determining this was not all just coincidence. Count to five, they asked. Five knocks on the walls. Count to fifteen. Fifteen knocks. This was not just the random scratching of animals or a tree limb being blown by the wind. Whatever was making these noises, it was most certainly sentient. Excited by their discovery, the sisters began to use a more complex system of communication, by going through the alphabet and having the spirit knock at the desired letter, to have full-fledged conversations with the spirits. Their parents were perplexed. They went to get the neighbors, who were able to act as witnesses and corroborate the sisters' stories later.

Eventually, the sisters were able to determine that the ghost was that of a murdered man, who said he was buried in their cellar.

The story grew from there. The murdered man was Mr. Charles

Rosna, a peddler killed by Mr. John Bell. The Weekmans, who lived in the home before the Fox family, said they heard rapping sounds too. As for the basement? Prompted by the girls' story, several people began to dig around in the cellar of the home—and indeed bones were found. (Cue Vincent Price music.)

And just like that, the Fox sisters became stars in the séance community and led the growth of the Spiritualist movement. Spiritualism developed into a minor religion in the US during the second half of the nineteenth century. It offered a more personal faith experience for believers, who participated in home séances with small groups of people instead of large church congregations. For believers, Spiritualism provided hope that they could communicate with their lost loved ones, which made it an important part of their mourning rituals, and it seemed to prove that there was an afterlife (or the "Summerland," as some called it), making it more palatable than rigorous fire-and-brimstone doctrines. As it attracted more progressive followers, including some Protestants, it was connected to other reforms of the period, such as women's suffrage, temperance, and abolition, and its devotees went on lecture tours and wrote pamphlets to spread the word. Unlike the later mediums they inspired, the Foxes didn't publish books or appear at conventions, but they were in high demand for séances, where they would call on spirits, who would rap and thump in reply. By the autumn of 1852, just a few years after the first rappings, Maggie and Kate Fox were financially secure on their own—and they were both still teenagers.

Following the Fox sisters' lead, more and more women became Spiritualist mediums, addressing social reforms through the spirits they channeled—spirits that manifested in a variety of ways, not just through the Foxes' rapping noises but also via trance speaking, automatic writing, and the production of ectoplasm, a filmy substance that would issue from the medium's mouth. These women were often very young. Flora Temple, a popular medium from Bennington, Vermont, was only fourteen years old when she took the Spiritualist stage, speaking in a trance in front of an audience of several hundred people. Cora Hatch was a mere eleven years old when she first took the stage in Lake Mills, Wisconsin. Not all Spiritualists were young, nor were they all women—but many of the most popular ones were in their twenties, if not their teens, and many were also attractive. The young Hatch, for example, was noted for her long, blonde hair, styled into ringlets. Her hair was written about almost as much as her abilities to channel the dead. Youth and beauty signaled innocence and virtue, which allowed these mediums to position themselves as conduits to the "other side" without any troubling whiff of witchcraft.

Traditionally in the Western world, "good" women are in the home. In the Fox sisters' day, this idea was expressed as the "angel in the house," a Victorian ideal of perfect femininity that originated with an 1854 poem by Coventry Patmore (inspired by his own wife, apparently).

Patmore was in turn inspired by centuries of Christian religion. The description of the perfect wife in Proverbs 31 sounds a lot like the angel in the house: She's hardworking (so long as she works in the home). She gets up while it is still dark and toils throughout the night by lamplight. She makes her children's clothing and the home's bedding. She's clever with money. She gives to the poor. She cooks for everyone. And for all of this—her husband is respected.

So "good" women are the house angels, working hard but working silently. They don't question their place or those in charge. They are sweet and smile so that they are something pretty to gaze upon. They never talk back. They never question. "Bad" women, by contrast, are brash and loud. They have ambition and (*gasp*) opinions on things outside of the home. They are witches. They are children of the Devil.

This is where Spiritualism is key in the progress of women's resistance to the patriarchy. Spiritualist mediums built businesses, made money for themselves, secured fame—all while maintaining the respectability of the "innocent woman" because they used the home to do their work. The Fox sisters in Hydesville in 1848 were kicking off a similar project to another that would be held a few months later and only twenty miles away: the Seneca Falls Convention, the first women's rights convention to be held in the States.

Eventually, Spiritualism experienced a backlash, largely from men who may have resented the way mediums were able to gain power through their supposed interactions with spirits. During Spiritualism's heyday and the transition from the use of the term *medium* to the more recognizable *psychic*, the majority of practitioners were women. It wouldn't take long, though, for investigatory groups to emerge and put the mediums to the test, often on stage in front of the public. This created a kind of gender divide in the occult world, as the investigators were often men, while the psychics were often women. (Some women did participate in such debunking, but we will discuss them in more detail later.)

The Fox sisters' celebrity didn't survive this skeptical resistance. In 1888, onstage at New York's Academy of Music, Maggie Fox confessed that their conversations with spirits were never real. She provided a demonstration of how, as younger girls, they had popped and cracked their joints to create the phenomenon of spirit raps. Kate corroborated the confession, and despite the fact that Maggie later tried to retract it, they both ended their lives in disgrace and dire financial straits.

Helen Peters Nosworthy

THE WOMAN WHO BUILT OUIJA

f there is one lesson that the horror movie has taught us, it's that the Ouija board is a doorway to the spiritual realm—and it is something not to be messed with! Movies such as *The Exorcist*, *Ouija*, *Paranormal Activity*, and *The Conjuring 2* all feature characters who play with the spirit board, only to be possessed and tormented by demons and evil spirits for the duration of the film. It makes for terrifying and tingling tension, but the board itself has its own fascinating history, with a woman at its center.

The so-called talking board emerged in the midst of the Spiritualist movement of the late nineteenth century as a useful tool for mediums contacting the other side. Prior to its popularity (and commodification by a toy company), different modes of consulting the spirits were used, from reading tea leaves to holding a pendulum. Rudimentary talking boards date back to the ancient world, but the talking board we now know as Ouija dates to the late 1800s. The first advertisements proclaimed it to be a link between the spirit world and the material one, providing answers with "marvelous accuracy" and "never-failing amusement." Visually, the talking board hasn't changed much from those early versions: they were flat rectangular boards with the words *yes* and *no* in the corners and, in the middle, the alphabet and the numbers zero through nine. Each set came with a teardrop planchette to guide the spirits as they answered questions. The boards marketed in the 1890s were made of wood, including the planchette, whereas today's versions typically are made from cardboard and plastic. They've also increased the price quite a bit; the original boards were advertised with a $1.50 price tag.

It only took a few years for entrepreneurs to begin to market these early boards to be sold directly to consumers for use in their own home. In 1890, the Kennard Novelty Company was formed to fill this niche market. The company designed its own board, complete with letters and numbers to aid the spirits, but it needed a unique brand for its new design.

Enter medium Helen Peters Nosworthy, the sister-in-law of Elijah Bond, one of the owners of Kennard Novelty Company. Unfortunately, not much is known about Nosworthy. The recorded history of Ouija includes the entire histories of the men who ran the Kennard company (and their dramas while keeping the business going), but not much has been preserved about her. We do know that she was considered a "strong medium," at least according to her brother-in-law Bond, which is perhaps why she was asked to help come up with a marketable name for this new talking board game. It was her idea to ask the board itself what it wanted to be named.

Nosworthy reportedly sat down with Elijah at the board and asked it what it should be called. The planchette began to move, and they watched as it slowly spelled out O-U-I-J-A. When they asked for clarification on what this meant, the board simply spelled out GOOD LUCK. (People often say that the Ouija name comes from the French and German words for *yes*, *oui* and *ja*, but the Kennard Novelty Company has never said this.)

To add to the lore surrounding the mysterious name, the owners of the Kennard Novelty Company said that the Ouija name was confirmed because Nosworthy was wearing a locket that day with a woman's picture and the name OUIJA printed inside. Most scholars think that Nosworthy's locket most likely contained a picture of the writer (and women's rights activist) Ouida, but that wouldn't be quite as eerie as the original story.

The Ouija board was a moneymaker for the Kennard Novelty Company, so much so that by 1892, the company expanded from its one factory in Baltimore to two factories. Then they added two more in New York City. The expansion continued so rapidly that year that three more factories were added: two in Chicago and one in London. The Ouija board was officially international.

The Ouija board continued to find success and transform into something of a cultural phenomenon. In May 1920, the *Saturday Evening Post* included a cover from Norman Rockwell, one of the best-known painters of American culture at the time, depicting a man and a woman consulting a Ouija board.

Today, Helen Peters Nosworthy is considered the mother of the Ouija board. In 2018, the Talking Board Historical Society paid tribute to her with a monument at Fairmont Cemetery in Denver, Colorado, where Ouija fans and history buffs can visit her gravesite. At the ceremony following the unveiling of her monument, a Ouija board was raffled off—a fitting tribute to the woman who named the famous board.

Art as Protest

THE OCCULT WORLD OF
· LEONORA CARRINGTON

In the mid-twentieth century, the occult seemed to be a perfect fit for the newest wave of feminist activism. It was a pushback against all the things conventional, conservative, Christian society valued—and that got attention. This new kind of occult activism also bled over into the art world, in particular in the work of artist Leonora Carrington. Carrington was born in England in 1917 and was a rebellious child, escorted out of two fancy European finishing schools before she found art. Her mother gave her a copy of Herbert Read's 1938 book *Surrealism* featuring a painting by Max Ernst on the cover. That same year Carrington went to a London showing of Ernst's works, and the two began an illicit (and famous) affair. She was nineteen. He was forty-seven and married. She ran away with him to France, despite the objections of her parents.

In Paris, the two became an integral part of the Surrealist art movement, throwing parties with the likes of Joan Miró, Pablo Picasso, and Marcel Duchamp. During these years Carrington's imagination took hold of her art. She wrote—plays, novels—and she painted. Then, politics and Nazis intervened. In 1940, Ernst had to make a quick exit rom France (both because he was a German and because he made unacceptable art—but there were also rumors of espionage), which he did with the help of Peggy Guggenheim, his wealthy patron. The next year, Ernst married Guggenheim, leaving Carrington alone.

For a while, her life was dark. She was even institutionalized in Spain and subjected to the electroshock therapy that was popular in the day. Pablo Picasso, though, saved the day, sort of. He introduced Carrington to Renato Leduc who was working for the Mexican embassy. Leduc helped Carrington escape the institution and get to Mexico—by marrying her. In Mexico, her career really ignited, even though she had a difficult time fitting in with the artists there (Frida Kahlo reportedly called Carrington and her friends "those European bitches"). The Mexican landscape offered fertile ground for Carrington's imagination. She began to study alchemy and a Mayan text, the *Popol Vuh*. She worked with local female healers, who taught her how to mix herbs. She also studied Robert Graves's book *The White Goddess.*

Her surrealism was a mixture of Irish fairy tales her mother told her as a child, Mayan religious images, and depictions of various goddesses as she imagined them. By the 1960s and '70s, her artwork became more political after she cofounded the Women's Liberation Movement in Mexico (the group made posters displaying Carrington's work). Today, her tarot-inspired works of art are still show

Pamela Colman Smith

Perhaps because it's so accessible—it's inexpensive and comes with easy instructions—tarot card reading is an especially popular form of occult dabbling. The internet has made a wide marketplace for all kinds of tarot, offering everything from unicorn-themed decks to illustrator Lisa Sterle's Modern Witch Tarot deck (whose cards feature drawings of women in modern dress) to *Labyrinth* decks for the David Bowie enthusiast. No matter what stokes your intuition, chances are there's a deck designed especially for you. Still, most consider the definitive tarot to be the Rider-Waite deck, so named for the famed mystic A. E. Waite and the publisher William Rider and Son.

Based on a long history of illustrated playing cards (used both for games and for telling the future), the Rider-Waite deck introduced the Major Arcana and Minor Arcana as we know them today. It is still the most popular deck, and the imagery and symbolism it introduced heavily influence the art of newer decks, even the *Labyrinth* one. But that imagery didn't come from the pen of Mr. Rider *or* Mr. Waite. It's the work of an extraordinary woman named Pamela Colman Smith.

Smith was the artist responsible for the cards in the Rider-Waite deck. Born to American parents, Smith spent her childhood moving between England, New York, and Jamaica, where she became enamored with the folklore of the island. She may have been biracial (some have suggested that she had Jamaican roots in her ancestry), and she certainly loved Jamaican culture, incorporating it into her art and her clothing style. Like her ethnicity, her sexuality is a subject of speculation. Plenty of accounts suggest that she was queer and that she preferred relationships with women. We're uncertain about these details in part, it seems, because Smith wanted it that way. Sexuality and identity were fluid for her. If someone asked whether she was Japanese, for instance, she might respond by creating a portrait of herself dressed in a kimono. As an artist, she seemed keenly aware that people viewed her as an other, and she wanted to explore what that meant.

In light of her obsession with art and folklore, her bohemian lifestyle was a given. She would often host writers and artists in her studio, holding salons to discuss whatever mystical philosophy was the topic of the day. Smith studied art in New York before moving to London, where she worked at the Lyceum Theatre. During her time there, Smith worked with Bram Stoker, author of *Dracula* (which was performed at the Lyceum as a play). She then teamed up with Stoker as illustrator of his 1911 book *The Lair of the White Worm*.

Working with writers turned out to be quite special for Smith, especially when she met William Butler Yeats, who was keenly interested in occult subjects (he was part of the Ghost Club that later included Algernon Blackwood, writer of weird fiction, among many others). It was Yeats who introduced Smith to the Hermetic Order of the Golden Dawn, which she joined in 1901. The Hermetic Order of the Golden Dawn was a secret society that explored aspects of the occult and the paranormal, as well as philosophy and magic. Members over time included Blackwood, as well as other creatives like Sir Arthur Conan Doyle (creator of Sherlock Holmes) and Arthur

Machen (a horror novelist best known for his 1890s novella *The Great God Pan*). Famed occultist Aleister Crowley also took part. In this group Smith met A. E. Waite. Smith followed Waite when he left the group to form his own offshoot, and it was then that he approached her about his idea for a deck of divination cards.

At Waite's urging, Smith took on the task of both reinventing old images and creating entirely new ones for his deck, including the backs of the cards, for which she received, according to her, "very little cash."

After completing her work on the deck, Smith faded from the occult scene. She converted to Catholicism, and though she continued to produce art, she had trouble selling pieces the way she used to. She died in London in financial trouble, and even her burial place is not known today. The tarot deck she created took on a name that left her out completely. She was seemingly erased from an enormous part of occult history.

Today, though, that is changing. Many tarot readers refuse to use a Rider-Waite deck out of protest. Others call it the Smith-Waite deck, to honor the woman who created their favorite tool. Many shops now carry the traditional deck with her name in bold letters across the cardboard box: "The Rider-Waite deck with illustrations by PAMELA COLMAN SMITH."

It's a start. Still, it is more than a bit frustrating that the occult society that seemed to welcome powerful women, women who left other religions, couldn't make a history or a legacy for one of its founding mothers.

If nothing else, we can say her name now.

Marjorie Cameron

M arjorie Cameron's life began in Iowa in 1922, and by all accounts, she was the rebel in the family. Desperate to escape her small-town life, she enlisted in the navy in 1940 as soon as she graduated from high school. She drew maps and worked with a photographic unit during World War II, and she found success in the armed forces—until she went AWOL after learning her brother had been injured. Following an honorable discharge in 1945, she moved to Pasadena, this time pursuing art and a more bohemian lifestyle.

That bohemian artsy life turned to the occult when Cameron met Jack Parsons.

A history of the occult in America would not be complete without Jack Parsons, though some might not recognize his name as readily as those of his colleagues Aleister Crowley and L. Ron Hubbard. Crowley is most notable for his philosophy Thelema, which became a major movement in occult religion. Thelema was built on the idea of ritual magick (Crowley's preferred spelling) and the basic belief of "Do what thou wilt." L. Ron Hubbard is, of course, the founder of Scientology. Before Scientology, however, Hubbard was a philosophical and spiritual scientist of sorts, working with Parsons and following the lead of Crowley in his magickal journey.

Thelema is a complicated system, one that borrows rituals and symbols from various occult traditions in the service of manifesting a practitioner's "true will," their ultimate purpose. Crowley claimed that his new philosophy was dictated to him by an angel. The simplified idea is that manifesting your true will, and then living in accordance with that will, is the most important pursuit and the ultimate goal of magickal practice. Thelemic ritual syncretizes a number of other occult traditions, incorporating Kabbalah, goddess worship, astrology, and Crowley's own inspirations. It also encouraged sexual experimentation.

Here's where a brief history of the time is crucial. Crowley was born in 1875 in England, which meant he was raised in a culture of Victorian sexual repression. Anything outside of a heterosexual marriage was considered unnatural by society—though it is important to note that this was mainly applied to women, specifically white women, who were expected to be pure and perfect wives. Of course, this idealized purity required the opposing concept of a "fallen woman," which led to the treatment of sexually promiscuous women as deviants. Prostitution was a major (though hidden) part of Victorian and Edwardian society, and sex workers often were subjected to forced examinations by government officials, a hotly debated practice that led some women to lobby for reform in how sex workers could maintain control over their own bodies in the face of government regulations.

This is a crash course in Victorian sexuality, of course, and it doesn't plumb the depths of feminist or queer identities as they were forming, and were lived, during this period. But this was a period of quick and major change in regard to the understanding of sexual identities. The earliest ideas of sex magick were also beginning to emerge, especially from the occultist and medium Paschal Beverly Randolph, whose rituals involving sex and the occult were published posthumously in *Magia Sexualis: Sexual Practices for Magical Power*. Then there were less occult sexual publications by Ida Craddock, who wrote about the importance of a healthy sexual relationship between husband and wife. Craddock's subject matter, sex within a monogamous heterosexual relationship, shouldn't have been particularly controversial even in the Victorian era, but her writings were considered obscene (maybe, at least in part, because of her gender) and she was imprisoned several times, including a stay in a mental hospital. Craddock's and Randolph's ideas on sex would play important roles in Crowley's ideas of sex magickal rituals, detailed in his 1912 *Book of Lies*, among other publications around the same time.

Some of Crowley's sexual rituals were solo (masturbatory), while others required consenting partners. This is where Marjorie Cameron entered the picture. Jack Parsons was already a Thelemite working with Crowley when he met Cameron. Parsons was a rocket engineer whose work with rocket engines is considered foundational—but he had more than a passing interest in occult experiments, too. Parsons, along with his first wife, joined the Ordo Templi Orientis (OTO), a Thelemic organization, where he investigated astral projection, astrology, demon summoning, voodoo, and magic based in the Enochian tradition (based on sixteenth-century writings), among many other subjects. His occult experimentations were widely known, and rumors that he was a "black magic" practitioner (and/or a spy) ruined his reputation in rocket-science circles.

Parsons's occult activity made an abrupt shift when he met Cameron. He'd been looking for some time for a figure known as the Scarlet Woman, whom many occultists (including Parson and Hubbard) believed was an incarnation of Babalon, a goddess written about in Crowley's Thelemic texts. Apparently, sex with Babalon would result in an elixir of life. We won't get into the details—but it involves fluids. It's also important to note that Babalon could come in many forms, which meant that many women were given this title, including Ruth Crowley, Aleister's first wife, and the poet Jeanne Robert Foster.

Together, the two men had been planning a series of occult experiments, beginning with those Enochian rituals that Parsons had prepped. Their goal was to bring about the Aeon of Horus, which Crowley wrote about. It was supposed to open a kind of vortex and welcome in a new time of enlightenment and self-realization. Now, they just needed to wait for the right woman to come along, who would be called forth by the ritual. Specifically, they needed a red-haired green-eyed woman to show up.

When Parsons met Cameron, he recognized her, with her fiery hair and piercing eyes, as the woman he had been waiting for, and for her part, she was immediately attracted to him. They began a sexual relationship, one that had personal meaning for the two of them but one that they believed also had a larger magickal meaning. The year was 1947. Parsons and Hubbard were planning to perform the Babalon Working, a ritual to bring the goddess to material form here on Earth. (Cameron was both Babalon in the flesh as well as the physical representation of Babalon, meant to facilitate the manifestation of the goddess.) The ritual itself was taken from a novel written by Crowley in 1917, called *Moonchild*. This is a quick rundown: through various sex acts, Parsons and Cameron, along with Hubbard, were supposed to bring about a child who existed only on the astral plane, and that child would usher the goddess into an earthly existence. Hubbard presided over the sexual acts and saw that all sex fluids and bloods were sufficiently mixed.

This was the second time that Parsons and Hubbard tried to complete the Babalon Working ritual. The first time was with Sara

Northrup (nicknamed Betty), the sister of Parsons's wife, Helen, whom he married in 1935. Betty and Parsons began an affair while Helen was away, and they grew closer through their occult experiments within the OTO. Betty was the first Scarlet Woman, but the ritual didn't work. The relationship between the magickal threesome became complicated when Betty and Hubbard began to see each other (Betty would become Hubbard's first wife when she married him in 1946).

Parsons was undeterred. He was convinced that Cameron was the true Scarlet Woman. On February 28, Parsons drove to the Mojave Desert and invoked the goddess, the final ritual, which he claimed was successful.

By today's standards, Cameron might seem like just an interchangeable part in all these shenanigans, a vessel for the magickal work. In fact, Cameron taking the role of the Scarlet Woman was sexually progressive for the time. Like many other occult experiments, this one was participating in sexual political rhetoric of the day, by promoting the idea that a woman could be in charge of her own body and have the power to choose her own sexual partners.

Successful or not, Parsons and Hubbard parted ways, in part due to Hubbard's relationship with Betty. Hubbard would go on to publish *Dianetics* in 1950, which would be a keystone text in Scientology. Cameron married Parsons in 1946 and then traveled to New York City, where she discovered she was pregnant and had an abortion. She then moved on to Paris, with the intention of pursuing an art career, but she found postwar Europe to be the wrong place for her. So, she made plans with Parsons to travel to Mexico in 1952. The night before their departure, tragedy struck: Parsons was killed in an explosion in his home laboratory.

In Mexico, a distraught Cameron attempted to contact the spirit of Parsons, her friend, husband, and lover. When she returned to California, she focused on her art and poetry. She also began a collaboration with the eccentric film director Kenneth Anger (who famously wrote the gossip book *Hollywood Babylon*). Cameron acted in Anger's 1954 film *Inauguration of the Pleasure Dome*, playing the roles of the Scarlet Woman and Kali. Later, when Anger spoke of Cameron, he described her as a woman with real occult power: "She was extraordinary—a genuine witch. She had powers. Unusual powers. Extra powers. She kind of knew things before they happened. She loved a full moon."

Her legacy was largely erased, eclipsed by bigger names in her story, like those of Parsons and Hubbard. When Parsons was investigated by the FBI for espionage charges late in his life, many blamed Cameron for her bad influence on him, and rumors swirled that she got him into the occult, specifically the "black magic" and "Satanism" that led to his poor reputation in the rocket-science community, despite the fact that he was already a member of the OTO when the two met.

Nonetheless, some—like Anger, who continues to speak on art and the occult—are still talking about her influence today.

Margaret Murray & Doreen Valiente

THE WOMEN BEHIND WICCA

Today, the word *coven* has been embraced by feminist groups, used anytime women get together in support and solidarity for one another. In its etymological history, the term has been used to describe specifically a gathering of women since the mid-seventeenth century, but it largely fell out of favor until one woman brought it back into the public lexicon. Margaret Murray was an archeologist (an Egyptologist, to be specific) who helped bring the idea of witchcraft to the masses, writing about it as a religion that was being practiced in remote parts of the world.

Murray was born in India in 1863 to a British family. As a child she was especially influenced by her mother, who often traveled—alone, which was highly unusual for a woman at the time—in her work as a missionary. Perhaps following her mother's model of female independence, Murray decided in her thirties to pursue a career in archeology, despite her lack of formal education. And she was largely successful, becoming the first female lecturer in archeology in the United Kingdom by 1898.

In the 1920s and '30s, Murray published two books, *The Witch-Cult in Western Europe* and *The God of the Witches*, and the entry on *witchcraft* in the 1929 *Encyclopedia Britannica*. In her work, Murray theorized that there were pre-Christian witch-cults engaged in fertility rituals in England and Europe that had gone underground after the witch hunts of the sixteenth and seventeenth centuries, or the "Burning Times" as subsequent followers of her theory would call them. She supported her thesis about pagan fertility cults partly with evidence from confessions coerced through torture from the accused women during witchcraft trials. In essence, she argued that when these women admitted to being witches and practicing witchcraft, they were telling the truth. Many of the aspects of the cults that Murray described became part of later pagan movements, including a coven, or group of witches with thirteen members, sometimes led by a high priest of sorts, who she said was interpreted as the "Devil" by Christians, and the identification of feast and ritual days organized by important points in the agricultural year such as Candlemas, Imbolc, and Lammas.

Today, Murray's work on this subject has been largely refuted by scholars, in part because modern historians are a bit more skeptical of information extracted through torture. But her books became extremely popular in 1950s England, as people looked outside organized religion for spiritual sustenance. One of the people who took Murray's ideas and ran with them straight into a new religious tradition was Gerald Gardner, the founder of the early version of what we think of today as Wicca, or the Craft. Although Gardner had been a civil servant in the English colonies, he considered himself to be an amateur anthropologist, with interests in Freemasonry, magic, and other occult systems. It's not surprising that he would be drawn to the idea of witchcraft. In his 1954 book *Witchcraft Today*, published after the 1951 repeal of England's Witchcraft Act of 1735, he disclosed his 1939 initiation into the New Forest coven and described what he saw as a continuing pagan tradition of a fertility cult carrying into the twentieth century. At this time, the New Forest coven was only rumored to have existed; no evidence had been discovered of its existence, let alone that Gardner had joined, and Gardner himself was coy about the details of an "old" religion in which he said he participated. He did spell out some aspects of the new religion he called Wica, which he suggested meant the "wise people."

In his description of the old religion and its practice, Gardner emphasized the Goddess as the primary focus of worship and connected her to life, fertility, growth, the seasons, and the moon. He noted the presence of the Horned God, or the consort of the Goddess, who is linked to animals and the process of death and rebirth and perhaps reincarnation. The God goes through the seasons with the Goddess; together, they enact birth, life, death, and rebirth according to the time of the year. According to Gardner, these cycles of the changing world are celebrated through rituals connected to the moon and the seasons, and this became the Wiccan idea of the Wheel of the Year and the sabbats. Gardner also wrote about the Great Rite, which he saw as a sexual consummation, literal or metaphorical, between the High Priestess and High Priest as the Goddess and God. The celebrants would form covens of twelve to thirteen people and use a ceremonial circle to contain and focus the energy they created. Gardner suggested participants be nude, but that's optional. (He also included the act of scourging, or self-flagellation, which pretty quickly fell away in the following years.) Each witch would need tools, such as a ceremonial knife, or athame, a censer and incense, a cord, candles, and anointing oil, among other sacred objects. The components of Wicca have evolved over the years, some parts fading out or changing, with later followers adding things as needed. Today, there is truly no one way to be a Wiccan.

Interestingly, Gardner took pains to emphatically assert that blood sacrifice is not required in any way. He insisted that witches should use their powers for good, which anticipated the idea of the Wiccan Rede: "An it harm none, do what ye will." This is why hexing is frowned upon. Hexes are intended to hurt people. The proper course of action is to bind someone so they don't hurt themselves *or* others.

Gardner effectively combined Murray's ideas with a lot of the occult information he was interested in, such as nineteenth-century Theosophy and Spiritualism, Aleister Crowley's magick, the Hermetic Order of the Golden Dawn, the initiation rites of Freemasonry (which he adapted for his brand of Gardnerian Wicca), and Charles Godfrey Leland's 1899 book *Aradia, or The Gospel of the Witches*.

Whereas Gardner is seen as the Father of Wicca, the High Priestess of the coven he founded, the poet Doreen Valiente, became known as the Mother of Modern Witchcraft. Valiente was born in 1922 in a suburb of London into a religious family. She rebelled against her Christian upbringing, going so far as to quit a convent school in her teens. Attracted to the occult at a young age, she had memories of psychic episodes that occurred when she was a child. This curiosity led her to read voraciously about witchcraft and paganism. There were rumors throughout her life that Valiente was a spy during World War II, even possibly working at Bletchley Park. This remained purely speculation, as she never addressed the topic.

Valiente began corresponding with Gardner in 1952. He initiated her into his coven, and by the mid-1950s, she was named the High Priestess. Her interests in writing, especially poetry, served her well in this position. She worked on Gardner's *Book of Shadows*, filling in gaps with more information, and she wrote a kind of liturgy for the new religion. Her "Charge of the Goddess," a liturgical text recited during Wiccan rituals, is still popular today, though the American feminist Wiccan Starhawk would revise it slightly in the 1970s, creating another popular version of the Charge.

Valiente's connection to Gardner did not last beyond 1957. In her 1989 book *The Rebirth of Witchcraft*, Valiente described the circumstances around a split in the coven, focusing on her and several other members' concerns that Gardner was seeking too much press attention and sharing too much information about the Craft. She also described a list of "Laws" that she and her allies believed Gardner drew up in response to their concerns. These laws instituted a more controlling top-down approach to the organization of the group. One law in particular bothered Valiente; it stated that the High Priestess should "recognize that youth is necessary to the representative of the Goddess" and, therefore, should "gracefully retire in favour of a younger woman, should the coven so decide in council." It's not surprising that after this experience Valiente would become a supporter of the Craft's connections to feminism. She offered this final take on the 1957 breakup of the coven: "We had had enough of the Gospel according to St Gerald; but we still believed that the real traditional witchcraft lived." Much of her work, both with Gardner and after her break from him, helped to grow the Craft, making it more accessible to larger audiences.

After her death in 1999, the Doreen Valiente Foundation was created in March 2011. It holds a collection of her occult objects and books. Through its connection to the Centre for Pagan Studies, the foundation educates the public about Valiente and the Craft by displaying her materials, maintaining an archive, and organizing public lectures.

"An it harm none,

do what ye will."

—The Wiccan Rede

Starhawk

Doreen Valiente saw the potential in the Craft for pursuing feminist and environmental aims early on, leading her to welcome the merging of Wicca and feminism that developed in the late 1960s and 1970s in the United States. Of course, there were other women in the following decades who expanded what it meant to be a feminist in the occult world. One of the most recognizable of these is Starhawk, but before her was Zsuzsanna Budapest, known as Z.

Budapest grew up in Hungary aware of a long family tradition of herbalism and witchcraft. When she moved to the United States, spending time first in Chicago and New York and ultimately landing in Los Angeles, she observed the patriarchal organization of her new country. In Los Angeles, she volunteered at the Women's Center, an organization that provided counseling and legal and medical services for women. After attending a women's liberation event, she joined the movement, and in 1971, she and a group of like-minded women began the Susan B. Anthony Coven No. 1. She worked to develop the feminist, or Dianic, form of Wicca, insisting on women-only covens (unlike Starhawk); she called the Craft "Wimmins Religion." Her belief that only women—which she interpreted as individuals assigned female at birth, excluding transgender women—should participate in rituals led to protests at a pagan conference in 2011. Today her narrow ideas about gender are controversial, but her work was very influential in the 1970s. In her 2019 book *Waking the Witch*, Pam Grossman writes, "Budapest sought to create a religion where the feminine experience was lauded above all else, her goal being to restore a matriarchal way of life across the globe."

Starhawk, born Miriam Simos in 1951, was another well-known member of the Craft who, over the course of her journey with Goddess worship and Witchcraft, connected with Doreen Valiente and Z Budapest. She wrote an influential revision of Valiente's "Charge of the Goddess" and continued in Budapest's path of feminist activism, albeit with her own developments along the way. She was a founding member of the 1970s Compost Coven on the West Coast, which she describes in her pivotal 1979 book *The Spiral Dance: A Rebirth of the Ancient Religion of the Great Goddess*. She was also a founding member of the Reclaiming community, which, according to its website, is a "community of people working to unify spirit and politics," with a "vision . . . rooted in the religion and magic of the Goddess, the Immanent Life Force." The members "see our work as teaching and making magic: the art of empowering ourselves and each other." Founded in 1980, Reclaiming has spread beyond its base in San Francisco to locations across the United States and abroad. Starhawk is connected, as well, to the Spiral Dance ritual, which has been celebrated every year at Halloween (or Samhain) since 1979. This ritual was originally scripted by Starhawk, but as she points out often in her writing, like all rituals, this one has adapted to changing circumstances over the years. Its purpose is to mourn and celebrate those who have passed on while simultaneously holding hope for the next generation and the future.

In the twentieth-anniversary edition of *The Spiral Dance*, Starhawk walks the reader through her developing ideas about the Craft and the Goddess and their connections to activism since the book's original publication. She laments the fact that resistance to the patriarchy is still necessary and tracks her activism from second-wave feminist protests such as Take Back the Night to more recent endeavors regarding environmental issues. Importantly, she rejects the Gardnerian heteronormative idea of male and female polarities and traces her shifts in thinking "toward a much more complex and inclusive view of gender and energy."

In *The Spiral Dance* Starhawk emphasizes the connections between the personal and the spiritual and political activism. Moreover, she takes a broader view of activism, regarding feminist protest in common cause with other progressive movements. She notes that "Pagans and Witches have accrued a proud record of involvement in feminist issues, gay liberation, and antinuclear, antiwar, and environmental campaigns." This openness to the political world around her has moved her to connect to the surrounding natural world as well. She identifies a developing thread in her spiritual journey toward a heightened awareness of and respect for the natural world: "My current passion is to integrate more closely the worship of nature with knowledge that comes from the observation of nature, and to infuse science, ecological design, and environmental activism with the deep connectedness that comes from acknowledging the sacred." As a result of this acknowledgment of the sacred, Starhawk disagrees with critics' view of witchcraft as evil or dangerous. For her, "Witchcraft is belief in the continuance of life, and the possibility of a truly life-serving culture." Her other books *Dreaming the Dark: Magic, Sex, and Politics* from 1982 and *Webs of Power: Notes from the Global Uprising* from 2002 further expand on her thoughts about the connections between Goddess worship and larger political movements, both local and global.

Like Gerald Gardner, Starhawk describes the story of the Goddess and her consort, the Horned God, and the progressions through the Wheel of the Year with its rituals and feasts devoted to agricultural and life cycles of birth, growth, and death. Unlike Gardner, she acknowledges the debate over the story's historicity. She treats it as a mythology for a belief system and notes that all religions create overarching creation narratives. She writes, "There is a mythic truth whose proof is shown not through references and footnotes but in the way it engages strong emotions, mobilizes deep life energies, and gives us a sense of history, purpose, and place in the world. What gives the Goddess tradition validity is how it works for us now, in the moment, not whether or not someone else worshipped this particular image in the past." With these words, Starhawk brings the Goddess movement of the 1960s and '70s into the contemporary moment in its active resistance to the dangers of patriarchal organized religions.

"Witchcraft is belief in the continuance of life, and the possibility of a truly life-serving culture."

—Starhawk

THE CRAFT AND
THE CRAFT

At the heart of the 1996 film *The Craft* is a coven of four girls: Nancy (played by Fairuza Balk), Bonnie (Neve Campbell), Rochelle (Rachel True), and Sarah (Robin Tunney). These girls have problems: Nancy has a difficult home life, which includes poverty and abuse; Bonnie is covered in scars following a fire and struggling with low self-esteem and painful experimental medical treatments to treat her burns; Rochelle is tormented daily by a racist bully. But they also have access to the fantastic power of witchcraft.

Sarah and Nancy and their coven use that power to fix their problems: Nancy gets money, Bonnie gets beautiful skin, and Rochelle gets to see her bully's blonde hair fall out in front of the other girls in gym class. They also experiment with changing their hair color and levitating each other—you know, what all witchy girls do at sleepovers. But the movie does something more interesting than depict stereotypical teenage girls. The coven makes a move for more power. They call the four corners of the earth and attempt to invoke Manon, the fictional deity of the film.

After she has gotten rid of her abusers and moved her mother and herself into a fancy condominium, Nancy becomes obsessed with Manon. She wants to "invoke the spirit," which is the film's coded language for making the ultimate power grab. Nancy's not interested in just making money or getting revenge anymore—she wants total dominance. And this is ultimately what brings her to the dark side; she kills Sarah's former love interest and turns the rest of the coven against Sarah. Sarah is able to defend herself and is triumphant in the end, binding Nancy's powers. The other girls lose their powers (that's what happens to mean girl bullies, after all) and go on their way, and Nancy ends up being institutionalized.

But what happened behind the scenes of *The Craft* made the film unique in the history of women's relationship to the occult. The filmmakers wanted to accurately represent teenage girls engaging in the occult, so they researched Wicca—in particular, Gardnerian Wicca—while they were preparing to film. Pat Devin, a practicing Wiccan, was hired by production as a consultant. It was Devin's idea to include the binding spell in the film's last act, rather than have Nancy die. The production team also used real occult books during filming, including *The Ceremonial Book of Magic* by Arthur Edward Waite (of tarot fame), which was read aloud by one of the characters.

Of course, the occult community didn't fully embrace the film. Some felt that it wasn't accurate enough in its portrayal (the witchcraft tradition was a bit vague, and the Manon god was a complete fabrication), and other critics worried that it might further harm the public's perception of occult traditions. But it also brought awareness of Wicca to a whole new generation of practitioners.

Carol P. Christ

THE GODDESS IS A FEMINIST?

n the late 1960s, throughout the 1970s, and into the 1980s, things began to change as Wicca became more tightly connected to the Goddess movement and second-wave feminism. And this shift to women's concerns links Wicca and neo-paganism back to the progressive work of Spiritualists and Theosophists of the previous generations.

In her 1983 essay "Women in Occult America," theologian Mary Farrell Bednarowski argues that women's participation in occult movements from Spiritualism to 1970s feminist witchcraft hinges on three factors: 1) a recognition that "male-dominated Western society" is fundamentally antagonistic to women; 2) a commitment to "reintegrate spirit and matter, mind or soul and body, experience and reason"; and, 3) a belief that women are "especially suited for the enterprise of restoring wholeness and balance to all the institutions of society." In other words, women come together in occult work because they consider the patriarchy to be a unique threat to world harmony and believe that women are best positioned to heal these wounds. Scholars Carol P. Christ and Judith Plaskow note in their 1979 book *Womanspirit Rising* that this work of questioning a patriarchal "God the Father" view of religion can be traced back to Elizabeth Cady Stanton's 1895 book *The Woman's Bible*. Christ and Plaskow write, "The project was a product of Stanton's firm conviction that the political and economic subordination of women has deep ideological and religious roots. The degradation of women is basic to the biblical view of creation and redemption."

Twentieth-century second-wave feminist scholars of theology took this a step further. For instance, Mary Daly focused on the oppression of women inherent in traditional Judeo-Christian religion and the need to move beyond it to something welcoming to women, especially in her books *Beyond God the Father: Toward a Philosophy of Women's Liberation* from 1973 and *Gyn/Ecology: The Metaethics of Radical Feminism* from 1978. According to Christ and Plaskow, Daly posited that the patriarchal language and symbols embedded in Western religions and the burden of sin placed on Eve in the creation story create a dangerous hierarchical worldview in which attributes identified as masculine are seen as superior to those identified as feminine. Moreover, this male perspective on religion not only relegates women to inferior positions, but also it can warp women's views of themselves and their own experiences.

One way to address this issue was for women to seek to connect to a Goddess, and the growth of Wicca at this time made it perfectly poised to meld with the theological and political ideas in the air. In her 1978 essay "Why Women Need the Goddess: Phenomenological, Psychological, and Political Reflections," Carol P. Christ argues that politics needs to take spirituality and religion into consideration and not be compartmentalized. She writes, "Because religion has such a compelling hold on the deep psyches of so many people, feminists cannot afford to leave it in the hands of the fathers." She points out that societies form around their dominant religious symbols, and when a society is controlled by patriarchal symbols, women's power is typically seen as illegitimate or dangerous. For Christ, the Goddess as a new symbol, in place of the God, affirms "female power, the female body, the female will, and women's bonds and heritage." She writes that her mission is to "show how Goddess symbolism undergirds and legitimates the concerns of the women's movement, much as God symbolism in Christianity undergirded the interests of men in patriarchy."

It makes a lot of sense why women interested in the Goddess would turn to neo-pagan and Wiccan groups. Christ argues that Goddess theology should not be as hard-line as God theology and should emphasize interpretation and community rather than strict explication, which is similar to the independence and flexibility granted to witches, either alone or in covens. In her 1979 book *Drawing Down the Moon*, journalist Margot Adler stresses this freedom within Wicca for self-definition several times, noting that, even if she lists different traditions and covens, she could never catalog all of the various permutations and adaptations. Indeed, she warns the reader that, by the time her book would be released, some of the groups she did identify could have ended or changed course.

A word of warning here: Christ's views of the Goddess as she relates to theology were groundbreaking in the 1970s, but today's feminists' views are evolving past her womb-centric language, which can be exclusionary. Still, it is worth looking at her ideas as part of the larger historical period. In much of her work, Christ posits that women's bodies—or, at any rate, bodies with uteruses—can be symbolized by the cycles of the moon, which can bring greater connection to the cycles and processes of life. She writes, "In the ancient world and among modern women, the Goddess symbol represents the birth, death, and rebirth processes of the natural and human worlds. The female body is viewed as the direct incarnation of waxing and waning, life and death, cycles in the universe." This symbolism is mentioned in pagan and Craft communities that link their meetings and rituals with phases of the moon. Further developing the connection to women, Christ brings up the life cycle of maiden, mother, and crone that Starhawk also describes in her work. These three types of women can carry negative connotations, especially the term *crone*, but for Christ, in connection with the Goddess, the three nouns can illuminate the trajectory of a woman's life. The maiden is the young girl; the mother is creative, though not necessarily of children, as work, art, and service can be productions of this mature phase; and the crone symbolizes age, wisdom that can be shared, and perspective. All three phases are interconnected.

Finally, Christ considered the bonds among women that could be strengthened outside a patriarchal system with its competition and hierarchies. While she focused primarily on mother and daughter bonds, this idea of women forming communities goes beyond parental relationships and is an important tie to the second-wave feminist movement. When the women's liberation movement was just beginning in the mid-1960s, women met in smaller consciousness-raising groups that ultimately led to protest and action-based activism. In the early meetings, however, women simply shared their experiences with one another, and they realized that they weren't alone in their struggles. All of them were facing similar oppressions from the larger society, including, to name a few issues, the threat of rape and domestic abuse, restricted opportunities in education and employment, and enforced ignorance of their own bodies and medical care. This bonding laid the groundwork for the movement to come, and these small groups led to more organized community education for women. (One direct result: the creation and publication of the 1970 book *Our Bodies, Ourselves*, a revolutionary compendium of shared knowledge about sexuality, reproductive health, and other issues relevant to women.)

Silver RavenWolf

THE RISE OF THE TEEN WITCH

Despite the warnings from hand-wringing adults, teenagers in the 1990s became increasingly interested in witchcraft, largely due to the explosion of young witches in popular culture. *Charmed*, *Buffy the Vampire Slayer*, *Sabrina, the Teenage Witch*, and *The Craft* depicted teenage girls and young women as powerful, in control of their own lives, and able to navigate the (often scary) world around them and still come out on top. Helen A. Berger and Douglas Ezzy, authors of the 2007 book *Teenage Witches: Magical Youth and the Search for Self*, explain the attraction that these teens had to the occult. Some didn't see a place for themselves in more traditional religions. Others, though—and this is what Berger and Ezzy saw much more often—had always held these beliefs, they just never had a name to put to them until pop culture provided one. Berger and Ezzy explain it this way: "Teenage Witches generally do not join a group but become Witches either on their own or with other novices. The mass media therefore becomes particularly important in the process of both learning about and being a Witch."

One of the ways teens were able to access information about witchcraft in the '90s, alongside the explosion of internet newsgroups and message boards, was through the books of Silver RavenWolf.

Since the early 1990s, RavenWolf has been a prolific author for the new-age publisher Llewellyn Publications. She was also one of the first practitioners of the Craft to pen books for teens and other young new witches, like her popular 1993 book *To Ride a Silver Broomstick: New Generation Witchcraft*, the beloved *Teen Witch: Wicca for a New Generation* from 1998, and the practical hands-on guide, with accessories, *Teen Witch Kit* from 2000.

Initially, the larger pagan community was supportive of her guidebooks, especially when her work became the target of fearful evangelical Christians who thought *Teen Witch* was a pathway to Satanism. According to Stephanie Martin, a researcher and former member of Silver RavenWolf's Wiccan community, there was some pushback against RavenWolf from those who were concerned that her guides offered less-than-adequate detail for beginners and who had anxieties about possible historical inaccuracies in her work. There were even more concerns when RavenWolf's *Teen Witch Kit* was released.

The kit contained instructions, salt, a spell bag, and several talismans, including a silver pentacle pendant and a cord. The box it was sold in could be turned into a makeshift altar. Some critics said the materials were cheaply made, while others said that these were not even appropriate tools for beginner witches. Martin, however, emphasizes that the main criticism was that the kit was all too commercial. RavenWolf was branded "$ilver RavenWolf" online, and there were accusations that she was chasing money at kids' expense. Moreover, critics worried that these books would convert teens without their parents' knowledge or permission and then leave them without the resources needed to grow in their practice. RavenWolf didn't face these attacks alone. Martin documents defenses from Wren Walker of Witchvox.com and Laurie Cabot (whom we'll meet in later chapters), as well as her publishers at Llewellyn. Later, in her 2003 book *The Ultimate Book of Shadows for the New Generation Soli-*

tary Witch, RavenWolf thanked Ronald Hutton, a noted scholar of witchcraft, for reviewing her book for historical accuracy, perhaps a step to forestall waiting critics.

Despite those controversies in the early 2000s, her work was highly influential. Many of today's practicing witches who were teens at the time identify RavenWolf's writing as the entry point to their newfound spiritual practice. Some have gone so far as to say that her books helped to save witchcraft from obscurity in the '90s, a particularly difficult time for the Wiccan community when new membership was down.

In addition to her influential writing career and elder position in the Wiccan community, RavenWolf was the founder of the Black Forest Clan. This group focuses primarily on Celtic and German gods in a combination of Wiccan and Pennsylvania Dutch powwow faiths. Powwow has often been compared to folk magic, as it involves rituals to cure people's illnesses and injuries. A powwow ritual usually includes a recitation (a blessing, prayer, or calling upon the Christian Trinity) combined with a common object and the number three (as three is an important number in the Christian Bible). RavenWolf's own practice of Wicca was greatly influenced by this Pennsylvanian heritage; she even wrote a book about it, *HexCraft: Dutch Country Magick*, in 1997. According to RavenWolf, the Black Forest Clan achieved "legal clergy status" in 2012, and there are offshoot clans and covens in at least twenty states and abroad. In addition to continuing the Black Forest Clan tradition, the covens also serve as training spaces for future clergy and leaders.

Today, RavenWolf blogs, makes spirit dolls, and runs an online store, the Whisper Magick and Spell Candle Company. When asked in 2018 about past controversies, RavenWolf responded, "There is always going to be a criticism of one's work because perfection is what we strive for—not what we attain—which is delightful! There is good debate, and then there are the nonsensical personal attacks that are a waste of everyone's time." It's a good reminder that the occult and Wicca are always evolving. Criticism and debate can help with this evolution, opening conversations and new ways of thinking about how to make the occult space more welcoming and ethical.

America's patriarchal society has often excluded women from sites of power and influence. We have been told we couldn't work outside the home, make our own fortunes, or participate in religious leadership. Even so, we have a history of rebels—women and gender-nonconforming people who were willing to step outside those carefully drawn boundaries and implement change. The Public Universal Friend was a resurrected prophet who completely reimagined humans' relationships to God and one another and anticipated our current deconstructions of proscribed gender binaries. Women like Pamela Colman Smith and the Fox sisters made career moves within the occult space, creating art and making money when they normally wouldn't have been able to. And later women, like Starhawk, wrote their ideas into new women-centric religions that engaged with the ever-changing feminist movement.

If these women designed a space for other women to gain power within the occult, should it be any surprise that it didn't take long for women to use that space to gain political power? In chapter two, you will see how women used their powers of astrology and mediumship to influence politics, even up to the highest position in the White House, as well as how some women mobilized the occult image as a tool in the revolution against patriarchy and restrictive gender norms.

2

THE SPIRITS
GO TO
WASHINGTON

POLITICIZING THE OCCULT

The history of women and the occult is the history of women in politics. In chapter one, we introduced the Fox sisters and their rise to prominence in the Spiritualist movement. One detail about the Fox sisters' story that is often overlooked is how Spiritualism grew alongside another movement: the rise of feminism in the United States. Just months after the Fox sisters reported their first rappings in Hydesville, New York, the Seneca Falls Convention was held in Rochester—less than twenty miles from Hydesville. Not only was this the first women's rights convention to be held in the states, but it also marked a shift in values for the country. Women like Amy Post, Abigail Bush, and Elizabeth Cady Stanton were meeting with people like Frederick Douglass and using their platform to speak out for progressive issues like gender equality and the abolition of slavery. The rise of Spiritualism coincided with one of the first times in American history that women consistently had a voice in front of large audiences.

Talking with the dead was an equal opportunity job. In the 2001 second edition of *Radical Spirits: Spiritualism and Women's Rights in Nineteenth-Century America*, historian Ann Braude noted that "mediums themselves hailed from varied class backgrounds, and mediumships sometimes served as a vehicle of upward mobility." And mediums were truly diverse. There were African American spiritualists. Spiritualists who served the wealthy elite. Spiritualists across the agrarian South, in places like Memphis and Mississippi. Spiritualists in the White House.

At its beginning Spiritualism was overwhelmingly white, but that changed as the religion grew in popularity. Unfortunately, as states doubled down on segregation in the post–Civil War period of the late nineteenth and early twentieth centuries, racial tensions developed in the National Spiritualist Association of Churches, which led to the National Colored Spiritualist Association breaking away in 1922. This split contributed to the development of Black Spiritual churches in the 1920s and '30s. It's unclear why the term *Spiritualist* shifted to *Spiritual*. Perhaps it was a way to circumvent negative perceptions of Spiritualists and mediums. Or it could have been a way to attract Christian members through the biblical allusion to John 4:24. One of the earliest leaders of this new movement was Mother Leafy Anderson, who expanded her Eternal Life Christian Spiritualist Church from Chicago to New Orleans and then throughout the South and Midwest. Although this was a new iteration of Spiritualism that incorporated many elements from several religious and spiritual traditions, Anderson's Spiritual churches continued to focus on resistance through political and social messaging. Many of the future leaders Anderson trained were Black women, including Mother Catherine Seals in New Orleans. Seals continued her work by opening her Temple of the Innocent Blood to all people—regardless of gender or race—as a form of resistance against oppressive societal structures like segregation.

The focus on underrepresented voices in the occult is not limited to Spiritualism. Women often turned to the occult—literally, "the hidden"—because it offered a sideways route into structures of power. Political power in the US has traditionally been held by white men. Deep fears come to the surface of the populace when a person of color or a woman runs for high office. Google "Nancy Pelosi witch" and you'll see images of the Speaker of the House in green face. Vice President Kamala Harris has been criticized for laughing too much. Harris's laugh was mocked in the media as a "cackle," earning her a comparison to the Wicked Witch of the West. Hillary Clinton, despite having been a First Lady and a senator, was criticized for having a voice too "shrill" to be considered presidential. These criticisms were related not to these women's ability to lead nor to their political talent, but to their expression of gendered behavior. Women are expected to be quiet, self-effacing caregivers. Even though homes these days need two breadwinners, women are discouraged from being too ambitious or too focused on their careers. With these unconscious narratives, the accepted message seems to be that just being a woman is a detriment to one's political career, or any goals outside the home for that matter.

This is nothing new. History shows a long line of women struggling to make their voices heard. With so many societal expectations accompanying what it means to be a woman, many women have used other means to voice their political ideas—without necessarily running for office. Mediums and clairvoyants such as Harriet Wilson and Victoria Woodhull, among others, used spirits to relay political messages in the nineteenth century. Mediums even conducted sittings in the Lincoln White House. During World War II, Dion Fortune used psychic defenses to try to protect Britain from Hitler's advances. Later, astrologers like Madame Marcia in the 1920s and Joan Quigley in the 1980s guided First Ladies (and sometimes presidents) in hiring, firing, and scheduling. Women even have used the occult to protest outright against the government. For example, in the 1960s, a group calling itself WITCH wore stereotypical black pointy hats and robes while they hexed the patriarchy. And in the twenty-first century, a group of protestors used social media to hex President Trump. Though these women acted through different means, they were all doing the same thing: using the occult to influence change in the political landscape.

Victoria Woodhull

FROM CHILD PSYCHIC TO FREE-LOVE POLITICIAN

The first woman to run for president of the United States of America got her start as a child psychic. On September 23, 1838, Victoria Woodhull (née Claflin) was born in Homer, Ohio. She attended school only for a few years, and even then, her education was sporadic. As a child, young Woodhull, along with her sister Tennessee, "Tennie," accompanied her father on a bit of a con tour. He had them act as child clairvoyants, selling their services as "fortune tellers" to anyone who would buy. The family also sold a variety of cure-alls and elixirs, with promises that they would alleviate all manner of illnesses and diseases. Their father's cons resulted in Tennessee being accused of manslaughter when a client died.

Woodhull's early life wasn't all parlor tricks, though. As a child she claimed that she could speak to the dead and had powers to heal the sick. At age fifteen, she married a man who turned out to be an alcoholic. She also had two children with him, a son and a daughter, which made things more complicated, to say the least. Still, she didn't let a difficult childhood and rocky early adulthood stop her from making her way in the world. As adults, Woodhull and Tennessee worked as medical clairvoyants, helping people identify mystery ailments and healing them with their spiritual gifts. By 1868, they were employed by Cornelius Vanderbilt, the extremely wealthy railroad and shipping magnate, who distrusted most doctors. Rumors abound that Vanderbilt had an affair with Tennie, but whatever their relationship, the sisters became wealthy from stock tips, eventually opening their own firm with Vanderbilt's money. Woodhull, Claflin, and Co. made Woodhull and Tennessee the first female brokers on Wall Street.

By 1870, Woodhull had dedicated herself to the suffragette cause, and to further the movement, she worked with the Equal Rights Party. In May 1872, she was nominated as their presidential candidate, with the abolitionist Frederick Douglass as her running mate. It should be mentioned that Douglass had no part in these plans. Still, she was the first woman to appear on the presidential ballot.

It should come as no shock that Victoria Woodhull was an unconventional woman. As such, she didn't aspire to maintain the "true womanhood" that was idolized by Victorian society, and thus she eventually lost the support of a large part of the Spiritualist community; some were thoroughly scandalized by her ideas on free love, which went beyond simply saying that women didn't need to be married (a radical, yet somewhat accepted, idea espoused by some Spiritualist women). She was sexually free, living at one point with her ex-husband and her lover in the same house, in what would be considered an open relationship today. Good for you, Woodhull. Let the others clutch their pearls.

Spiritualism owed much to the philosophies of Emanuel Swedenborg, a Swedish religious leader who often spoke in trances. He claimed to have visions of angels giving men permission to have multiple wives and concubines. How convenient for the men (Swedenborg himself remained a bachelor). Because of Swedenborg's popularity in the Spiritualist community, his ideas became the basis of an argument for redefining sexuality and free love (for men, anyway) and helped to change the strict adherence to monogamy and marriage, at least a little bit. Still, sexual liberation wasn't available to women.

Nor were the feminist activists of the time prepared, for the most part, to fight for sexual freedom. The National Woman Suffrage Association, led by Elizabeth Cady Stanton and Susan B. Anthony, fought for equal partnership in marriage and for divorce laws that protected women. This seems to be as far as their idea of "free love" would go. It simply meant that women had equal rights to men in marriage and divorce—and that women were no longer property in a marriage contract. Woodhull, however, had different ideas.

Here's a description of one infamous night of revelry at New York's French Ball in 1869, held in the Academy of Music and put on by the Société des Bals d'Artistes, a night for the *demimonde* to live it up with the moneyed society—in other words, for the wealthy men and women of NYC to go wild with the prostitutes of the city. Everyone wore revealing costumes (sexy ballerina was a popular one) and donned masks. Woodhull and Tennie arrived around midnight, appropriately concealed in satin masks. So many women and playboys were in Woodhull's opera box that they spilled out over the balcony, which was described in detail by the papers: "There is not a whisper of shame in the crowd, it is now drunken with liquor and its own beastliness. It whirls in mad eddies round and round." The dancing was reportedly "wild and orgiastic." Later accounts said the evening was "no longer a dance at all, but a series of indecent exposures, a tumultuous orgy in which one man is struck by an unknown assailant, and his cheek laid open with a sharp ring, his white vest and tie splashed with blood."

A wild night, indeed. Woodhull was an early proponent of destigmatizing sex work, having said many, many times that "if women cared to sell their bodies it was better than the slavery of marriage." Still, she insisted that women knew what they were getting into, should they enter this kind of nightlife. Two schoolgirls attended the French Ball, and this concerned Woodhull greatly. She and Tennie had seen the girls that evening, being given drink after drink by Luther Challis, a Wall Street broker, and one of his wealthy friends, Charles Maxwell. Victoria followed up and found that the girls had been raped in a brothel, so she wrote about the horrible event in the November 2, 1872, issue of her paper, *Woodhull & Claflin's Weekly:*

> *[The girls] were seduced by [these men]. . . . They were taken to a house of prostitution, then they were robbed of their innocence by each of these scoundrels, Challis and 'Smith,' taking them to himself. And this scoundrel Challis, to prove that he had seduced a maiden, carried for days on his finger, exhibiting in triumph, the red trophy of her virginity. After three days these Lotharios exchanged beds and companions and when weary of this they brought their friends, to the number of one hundred and over, to debauch these young girls—mere children.*

The result of their shocking expose? Woodhull and Tennie were arrested and taken to the Ludlow Street jail for publishing pornography, for the use of the phrase "the red trophy of her virginity."

Harriet E. Wilson

ATTACKING RACISM THROUGH
NOVELS AND SÉANCES

arriet E. Wilson was a free Black woman born in New
Hampshire. She was also one of the first published Black
novelists in America; her 1859 novel *Our Nig; or Sketches
from the Life of a Free Black*, was based largely on her own life and
dealt with racism in America, specifically the northern states, before
the Civil War. By all accounts, Wilson was a resourceful woman. She
began writing as a way to address issues of race but also as an income
source, after her husband left her a single mother. She also worked as
a seamstress and sold hair products to provide for her family. Wilson first became involved with the Spiritualist community in the
early 1860s while working as a servant on a farm, eventually moving
to Boston, where she is listed as "the eloquent and earnest colored
trance medium" in the *Banner of Light*, a Spiritualist newspaper.

Wilson was also a part of the Massachusetts Spiritualist Association. In 1867, she participated in at least one of their conventions,
speaking at the same podium as the so-called Poughkeepsie Seer,
Andrew Jackson Davis. Her speeches usually covered labor reform,
but she also spoke about the importance of educating children in
Spiritualism. She continued to speak at public events for the next
few years. Not much is known about her work as a "trance medium"
or "trance reader," as she was sometimes called. (Usually, a trance

medium was someone who channeled messages from the spirit world using their own brain, without the use of spirit boards, séance tables, or other objects; they may not have gone "into a trance" as you might picture it—a woman's eyes rolling back in her head as a spirit possesses her and speaks through her voice—but instead often remained conscious.) Later in her career, records have her listed as "Dr. Harriet Wilson." She worked for a time as nurse, assisting a physician, and as a "clairvoyant healer."

Wilson was not the only Black woman who achieved fame as a medium (and writer) during the post–Civil War era. Born to a free family in Pennsylvania in 1795, Rebecca Cox Jackson reportedly had visions as a child. But as an adult, she had a religious awakening. She was working as a seamstress, married to Samuel Jackson, when God spoke to her—and taught her to read and write, even though her husband had refused to teach her. So she divorced her husband and became a Shaker with Rebecca Perot, her lifelong friend and companion; they became known as "the colored Rebeccas" in the Shaker and Spiritualist communities.

Jackson's writings were collected in the 1881 book *Gifts of Power*. These writings detail the "invisible spirits" who communicated with her on a regular basis. Jackson firmly believed that her ability to talk to the dead and spirits on the other side was evidence of her devotion to God. She claimed that she read only the Bible for years and regularly communicated with God. Wanting to reach more of the Black community, the two Rebeccas settled in Philadelphia and established their own Shaker "family" in a house on Erie Street, preaching to a largely female audience (though there were men too). What became known as "Mother Jackson's colony" survived for forty years following Jackson's death. Perot took the name "Rebecca Jackson Jr.," or sometimes "Mother Rebecca Jackson," following Jackson's death in 1871 and continued their ministry.

Spiritualism as a belief system was explicitly abolitionist, but white mediums—and the majority of high-profile mediums were white—sometimes used their séances to promote pro-slavery views. As Casey Cep wrote in May 2021 in the *New Yorker*, regional differences before and after the Civil War affected how spirit communicators portrayed ghosts of color in their séances: "Mediums with abolitionist sympathies passed on the stories of tortured slaves, while pro-slavery Spiritualists delivered messages of forgiveness from the same population and relayed visions of an afterlife where racial hierarchies were preserved." White mediums were also notorious cultural appropriators, calling on Native American "spirit guides" but rarely seeking approval or even communicating with living Native people whose spirituality they supposedly revered. As Cep points out, it may seem strange to talk about "spirits of color," but these guides were cartoonishly racialized, "conjured with exaggerated dialects for audiences at séances and captured in sensational costumes by spirit photography."

For Black mediums like Wilson, though, communication with spirits was (perhaps ironically) a way to make their own voices and experiences heard. In the next three decades, Wilson gave lectures to large Spiritualist audiences (some with attendance in the thousands), speaking out against racism, often in a trancelike state. By August 1873, Wilson was invited to speak alongside Victoria Woodhull to an estimated 16,000 people at the Fourth Annual Spiritualist Camp Meeting at Silver Lake, Plympton, Massachusetts.

Speaking the Truth

SOJOURNER TRUTH'S LANGUAGE AND
THE POWER OF TRANCE MEDIUMSHIP

The former enslaved woman Sojourner Truth has claimed a place in history as an outspoken abolitionist and suffragette. Truth wasn't a medium though she did live for a time in a Spiritualist community called Harmonia. But from examining her most famous speech, we can learn something about why Black women of her time were drawn to mediumship.

On May 29, 1851, in Akron, Ohio, Truth gave a speech that is still studied today, known as "Ain't I a Woman?" In it Truth makes the argument that she can do anything a man can do and therefore should be offered the same rights. She goes on to say that the savior of the world (in the Christian tradition) was brought about by God and a woman—man had nothing to do with it.

The speech was widely published, even immediately after Truth delivered it. One early version, transcribed by journalist Marius Robinson, was published on June 21, 1851, in the *Salem Anti-Slavery Bugle*. Robinson wanted to offer as complete as possible a transcription of Truth's speech and reportedly checked his version with her. Here are the first few lines of Robinson's transcript: "May I say a few words? I want to say a few words about this matter. I am a woman's rights. I have as much muscle as any man, and can do as much work as any man." The phrase "ain't I a woman?" is nowhere to be seen. Rather, Truth relies on the repeated phrase "I am a woman's rights."

So why was the change made? Scholars believe that people changed Truth's wording to embody the vernacular that white society would have expected from a former enslaved person. The revisions were rampant and often offensive. In one instance, social reformer Frances Dana Gage republished Truth's speech in the *New York Independent* on April 23, 1863, in openly racist dialect: "Dat man ober dar say dat women needs to be helped into carriages, and lifted over ditches, and to have de best place eberywhar. Nobody eber helps me into carriages or ober mud-puddles, or gives me any best place. And ar'n't I a woman?" Truth could not prevent the media from twisting her diction to suit the expectations of white audiences.

This may also be why many African American women used tools such as trance speaking, in which the medium goes into a semiconscious state to allow a spirit to speak through her, to disseminate their antislavery ideas. Trance speaking allowed women like Truth to communicate with a white audience without mediation, using their intellect and logic. These messages may have been easier for the white audience to accept if its members believed that the words were channeled through some kind of spirit trance and not coming directly from a Black woman.

Mother Leafy Anderson & Mother Catherine Seals

LEADERS OF THE BLACK SPIRITUALIST MOVEMENT

Mother Leafy Anderson was a founder of what became known in the 1930s as the Spiritual religion in New Orleans. She initially founded her Eternal Life Christian Spiritualist Church in Chicago in 1913, but after a few years, she moved to New Orleans to continue her work. Mother Anderson presided over a large congregation that included African Americans and whites, many of them paying customers, because Anderson insisted on the value of her services and charged for sittings, readings, healings, and training classes. Your money got you entertainment, though, not just sermons. Anderson was well-known for incorporating jazz music in her weekly meetings, including the song "When the Saints Come Marching Home." She taught healing and prayer, and she ended her services with a segment called the "Phenomena," in which she would select people from the audience and tell their futures or give them messages from beyond. This séance-like aspect, carried over from Spiritualism, would gradually fade out after the Spiritual religion became more religious and less concerned with spirits.

Anderson had a few spirit guides, or controls, including her mentor from Chicago, Father Jones; the Sauk warrior Black Hawk;

another Native American she called White Hawk; the Virgin Mary; and, later in her career, Queen Esther. Her guides were diverse, including men, women, African Americans, Native Americans, and historical figures from the Bible. Black Hawk, however, became her signature guide, and his presence continued into the twenty-first century in New Orleans Spiritual churches. White mediums, too, frequently employed Native American "guides," appealing to an image of Native people as spiritual forebears. This mirrored the popular myth of the "Vanishing Indian"; Native Americans in fiction were being increasingly portrayed as ghosts, as part of the American past. This was represented as a noble past, but one that was destined, nonetheless, to move aside as the United States fulfilled its manifest destiny. For Anderson, though, her Native guide may have had another layer of significance. Black Hawk fought against the government of the United States over the loss of his people's land; therefore, he could be a symbol of survival and of resistance to oppressive structures. Anderson used Black Hawk as a kind of patron saint for social justice.

Anderson's obituary listed her birthplace as Wisconsin, which could explain her interest in Black Hawk, and a student of Anderson's reported that she claimed partial Mohawk ancestry. But her descendant Bishop Edmonia Caldwell told a researcher that Anderson was actually born in Virginia, moved to Chicago and then to Raceland, Louisiana, before moving back to Chicago one more time prior to her final return to Louisiana and residence in New Orleans. She most likely encountered Black Hawk's spirit in Chicago, but no hard evidence survives of when and how.

Regardless of how she connected to Black Hawk, Mother Anderson was a tireless organizer. She planted the seeds of several southern congregations of her Eternal Life Christian Spiritualist

Church during her travels and eventually led an association that comprised not only the New Orleans congregation but also those from across the South and Midwest, including Chicago, Houston, Little Rock, Memphis, and Pensacola. When she passed away in 1927, her last words were "I am going away but I am coming back and you shall know that I am here." Indeed, when Zora Neale Hurston attended church services in 1928, she recorded that "the spirit of Mother Anderson" was in attendance. In addition to her work organizing and growing her church focused on spirit and justice, Anderson also had an eye on the future. She trained numerous students, many of them Black women who continued her legacy.

One of these students was Mother Catherine Seals, who, in 1922, started the Temple of the Innocent Blood in the Lower Ninth Ward of New Orleans. Mother Catherine Seals was born Nanny Cowans in 1897 and grew up in Kentucky. After moving to New Orleans, Cowans suffered violent physical abuse at the hands of three consecutive husbands. As a result of an assault by her third husband, Cowans became ill and suffered paralysis. When she visited a white faith healer for help, he turned her away because she was not white. At this point, Cowans turned to prayer and met a spirit. She then studied with Mother Anderson so she could start her own church under her new name: Mother Catherine Seals.

She proceeded to purchase a block of land on the edge of town and build her Temple of the Innocent Blood. This was a type of walled compound with two buildings, a small private temple and a large open-air "manger" that could hold an audience of three hundred or more. The location and design of the compound were a result of the radical nature of Mother Seals's work. She was a Black woman and, moreover, was welcoming all ages, genders, and races to her church—not a neutral thing to do during the Jim Crow era. The walled temple in an inaccessible part of the city would have felt safer for Seals's integrated congregation than would have a more central and more easily scrutinized location.

Mother Seals's open-door policy and healing mission were influenced by her life experiences. She took special care to aid women and children who had been abused or abandoned, and this focus inspired the name of her temple. *Innocent blood* referred to children of all races who—like Jesus—were born out of wedlock, often suffering abuse and neglect (along with their mothers) because of it.

Not everyone in the larger New Orleans community welcomed this help. The temple was the target of numerous arson attempts. Nevertheless, Seals persisted in her ministry, overseeing her church until her death in 1930, when thousands of people attended her jazz funeral, one of the largest in the city's history. Although Seals's successor, Mother Rita, was unable to keep the temple operating for long, Mother Seals's spirit, like that of Mother Anderson before her, was kept alive at meetings of Spiritual churches for years to come.

ARE YOU A GOOD WITCH OR A BAD WITCH?

Metro-Goldwyn-Mayer's 1939 adaptation of L. Frank Baum's 1900 book *The Wonderful Wizard of Oz* is an important moment in the representation of the witch in popular media. According to Pam Grossman, who wrote *Waking the Witch*, Baum, who was a proponent of women's rights, was likely partly inspired in his vision of witches by the views of his mother-in-law, Matilda Joslyn Gage, a suffragist with an interest in theosophy. Gage was of the opinion that the broad Christian church, as a patriarchal institution, hunted and executed alleged witches in the sixteenth and seventeenth centuries because it found them threatening. This may have inspired Baum to invent Glinda, the first good witch in popular culture.

Glinda is portrayed in the movie in a soft light wearing a glittery pink ball gown. Her favorite form of transportation is a bubble—no evil witch would use a bubble! And she giggles rather than cackling. Glinda seemed to be an entirely new creature altogether. She was a witch, but she wasn't evil. Glinda guides Dorothy and keeps her safe, but also lets Dorothy learn her own lessons and make her own way. Glinda is a powerful woman. She rules part of Oz, and the Wicked Witch of the West does not intimidate her.

But there were *two* witches in the film. Audiences thrilled to Margaret Hamilton's portrayal of the green-hued Wicked Witch of the West with her traditional witchy garb, broomstick, exuberant cackle, and wild pyrotechnics. And we all know people (maybe ourselves) who can remember their fear of her *and* her flock of flying monkeys that surrounded her castle on the outskirts of Oz. After the death of her sister and the loss of the ruby shoes to Dorothy, the Wicked Witch of the West vows vengeance on the girl from Kansas and her little dog, too (no more grievous offense can be committed than harming a dog). The Wicked Witch of the West would seem to be a continuation of the fairy-tale witch-as-evil-hag trope. But she's not that simple. She is independent, she is powerful, and she knows it. She has evil schemes, which she gleefully plans while wiggling her bent and bony fingers. Dorothy, by contrast, is an interloper who inadvertently fell into a dispute among witches when her house crashed into Oz.

After *The Wizard of Oz* and Glinda, the witch got a glow-up in the public eye. Over the next three decades, the witch began to look much different from the old woman in the gingerbread house from the Grimms' story. Witches transformed into sexy and beautiful seductresses or "normal" housewives. But whether they were prowling outside the home until domesticated by marriage or cooking a meal within it, women with magical powers were still viewed as a threat to the patriarchal status quo.

Madame Marcia

POLITICAL PSYCHIC ADVISOR
AND HOUDINI'S NEMESIS

As the personal astrologer to two First Ladies (Edith Galt, who married President Woodrow Wilson, and Florence Harding), Madame Marcia Champney once claimed that she was "at the hub of power of the government." According to Florence Harding's biographer Carl Sferrazza Anthony, Madame Marcia was known for predicting President Garfield's assassination, Edith Galt's rise to First Lady, and Warren Harding's seemingly long-shot presidential primary win. In 1920, Madame Marcia predicted President Harding's death to journalist Harry B. Hunt. This wasn't the first time she had done so; she began predicting to Florence before Warren won the primary that he would die in office. When President Harding's health took a dangerous turn in 1923, Hunt spoke with Madame Marcia again, and she predicted the president's passing almost to the day. As a result, she ended up being a suspect in popular conspiracy theories about the president's death. (She wasn't alone, however; there were enough theories about the muddled circumstances of his demise to target all the major players in the president's inner circle.)

The madame's powers of prediction made her a central power broker. According to Anthony, Florence Harding initially consulted Madame Marcia on a lark. She didn't even use her real name, going by the code name Jupiter for a long time as a test of Madame Marcia's powers. It's hard to believe that Madame Marcia wouldn't know who her client was before she revealed herself, however, if we take into consideration Madame Marcia's central location in DC's Dupont Circle and her expansive political connections. These political connections were why Florence Harding became interested in Madame Marcia; if the Washington rumors were to be believed, everyone was consulting the astrologer—from First Lady Edith Wilson to Supreme Court justices.

By the time she was an astrologer to the upper crust, Madame Marcia had come a long way from her roots. Born in Brooklyn in 1867, she spent her childhood in poverty, her father having abandoned the family. She claimed to have learned fortune-telling from a local elderly woman who "looked like a witch." She supported herself with these skills and worked in vaudeville until she married Horace Marion Champney in 1890. Within a couple of years, Horace left her to support herself, her mother, and two children on her own. To do this, she grew her occult business, while also taking on work in sweatshops when she could get it. At first, she did tarot, palm, and tea readings, but Anthony suggests that she felt she needed to up her game to gain better, more well-heeled customers. She expanded her work to include clairvoyance and astrology, and with a few correct predictions about crimes of the day that gained her notoriety, her business boomed. After adding Spiritualist minister to her résumé, she moved her family to Washington, DC, in 1909.

Once she moved to DC, she created a network of clients in the upper political echelons, whose queries and gossip most likely aided her powers of clairvoyance. By 1926, she had been a regular visitor to the White House while in the confidence of two First Ladies. And her involvement moved beyond simple predictions. Florence Harding used Madame Marcia's astrological readings and clairvoyance to schedule her husband's meetings, events, and travel. According to Madame Marcia, when Florence worried about blackmail by the president's mistresses, or became paranoid about the machinations of political enemies, or worried about betrayal by allies, she consulted her astrologer.

Her political influence—and probably her gender—made Madame Marcia a popular target for debunkers, including stage magician Harry Houdini, who was a committed skeptic and investigator of supposed psychic phenomena. Houdini and Madame Marcia faced off at the congressional fortune-telling hearings of 1926, which were the result of a bill proposed by New York congressman Sol Bloom that would "make fortune-telling a crime—punishable by up to a $250 fine and/or six months imprisonment—within the capital district." Houdini became involved when he pushed for Spiritualism to be included in the legislation, while Madame Marcia and minister Jane B. Coates led their compatriots to argue that it should be protected as a religion.

Houdini was committed to rooting out frauds, but he also seemed to be motivated by a suspicion of women specifically. He regularly accused mediums of being sexually licentious and immoral; for instance, in writing about the debunked medium Eusapia Palladino he asserted that she used her physical overtures toward male sitters to distract them from her sleight-of-hand maneuvers. At every turn, Houdini focused on the dangers of women refusing to act in ways that were socially defined as feminine—which is to say, pure and passive. Moreover, he framed his own performances as paeans to masculinity. Houdini shifted from an early act with his wife that borrowed from Spiritualism to his famous spectacle show as "The Handcuff King," which focused on his masculine strength, agility, and ability to escape being chained or bound. He represented himself as the opposite of these dangerous mediums and astrologers. Dare we say they offended his "manly virtue"?

It's not surprising that most commentators use the term *circuslike* to describe the atmosphere of the fortune-telling hearings. There was a great deal of animosity between Houdini and the mediums who were present, especially Madame Marcia and Coates. Houdini believed the mediums were perpetuating fraud and profiting from it. The mediums knew Houdini was threatening their livelihoods and, for the true believers among them (like Anna Louise Paine Fletcher, the Spiritualist wife of Senator Duncan Fletcher of Florida), their religious freedoms. All parties involved were adept at showmanship and performance, and thanks to the presence of journalists the proceedings became a sensational event. Every time a hint of a connection between mediums and astrologers and politics surfaced in the hearings, headlines spread across the country.

Some of this sensational media material came from the testimony of Houdini's crack investigator Rose Mackenberg (whom we will learn more about later). Her disclosure that she had attended readings in disguise with Madame Marcia and Coates rocked the room. Her testimony contained many shocking details, including descriptions of the sexual improprieties of the many mediums she had investigated undercover in her debunking career. Mackenberg also claimed that Coates and Madame Marcia told her that lawmakers were regularly seeking guidance from mediums and that séances were still being held in the White House. This was particularly irritating for the Coolidge administration, which had been trying to leave Madame Marcia's involvement with the Hardings behind. For their part, Coates and Madame Marcia denied having made the political claims to Mackenberg.

Madame Marcia and Coates were able to turn the tables on Houdini, however, by emphasizing the Christian religious and domestic aspects of Spiritualism and moving it from the occult realm to the realm of faith and the family circle. Testimony from Fletcher, a known quantity in Washington political circles, helped with this shift. The mediums also questioned Houdini's morals, his religion, and his very Americanness. To rebut this argument, Houdini called his wife, Bess, to the stand to affirm his connection to the status quo. Historian Jeremy C. Young notes that this move was "an effort to reestablish his masculine authority by demonstrating the gender hierarchy of his marriage." Houdini's wife agreed with him that he was not "brutal" in their marriage and that he was a "good boy."

While the mediums won out in the end, successfully arguing that Spiritualism should be protected as a religion, this hearing can be seen as a major moment in the ongoing conflict between the occult community and skeptics who question whether or not occult practitioners are engaging in fraud. It also was a key moment in the debate over the presence of occult practices in politics, a debate that didn't end in the 1920s with the election of Calvin Coolidge to the presidency.

Dion Fortune

THE WOMAN WHO DECLARED A MAGICAL WAR ON HITLER

Dion Fortune was an occult novelist and a practicing magician, and thus someone who turned the occult into both a creative pursuit and a source of personal power. Born Violet Mary Firth in 1890 in North Wales, Fortune made a career in the relatively new field of psychology, despite a lack of formal education. A voraciously curious woman, Fortune was also interested in the mythology surrounding King Arthur, British history, and Spiritualism. She took those interests and forged a new belief system, one that seemed uniquely "her." In the earliest days, for instance, she combined Christian mysticism with rituals that incorporated the mythology of the Holy Grail. Her books, like *Sane Occultism* and *Psychic Self-Defense* (from 1929 and 1930 respectively), were widely read and garnered Fortune a sizable following. Fortune, in her nonfiction, aimed for practical teachings and advice. In *Psychic Self-Defense*, for example, Fortune details how to safeguard oneself against all manners and modes of negative psychic energy, including attacks from psychic vampirism and hauntings. It's still considered a classic among esoteric knowledge seekers.

Fortune's occult interest led her to become a renowned teacher and an occult philosopher in her own right. After she joined the Hermetic Order of the Golden Dawn, she renamed herself Dion Fortune, a name formed from her personal motto, "God not Fortune." The order required initiation, but it was one of the few secret societies that admitted men and women equally. There, initiates like Fortune would have studied tarot, alchemy, and astral travel, just to name a few subjects. If you are imagining a kind of grown-up Hogwarts in real life, we are too, but the Order was more about ceremonial magic. Among the initiates were Irish poet William Butler Yeats, writer Arthur Machen, and infamous occultist Aleister Crowley.

Fortune founded the Fraternity of Inner Light in 1924, after a falling-out with the Golden Dawn, though she did get their consent to form her own group. It still operates in the UK today as the Society of Inner Light. The society, which uses Fortune's books *The Mystical Qabalah* and *The Cosmic Doctrine* as its core texts, offers admission to those who pass a study course. In addition to work with the society, Fortune also wrote novels, many of which have a magical or occult bent to them. *The Sea Priestess* is one of her most famous works of fiction, and it is still in print today. The novel follows the adventures of Vivien, who on her journey to spiritual enlightenment discovers a connection to Morgan Le Fay, Merlin, and Atlantis.

Perhaps more fascinating, though, is what Fortune chose to do with her occult power. In short, she mobilized a group of like-minded occultists to wage war against Adolf Hitler and the Nazi regime. The way she saw it was that the world needed defending, so she was going to use every tool at her disposal, even if that meant fighting on the astral plane.

During the tumultuous years of World War II, Fortune mobilized her group of devotees to psychically defend Britain against the Nazis. She began a letter-writing campaign in 1939, encouraging her friends and followers to join her in a kind of spiritual warfare against the evil in the world. On October 9, 1939, Hitler formally made parts of Poland part of his German Reich. On the same day, Fortune wrote this: "The Fraternity of the Inner Light has for one of its rules the avoidance of all participation in politics, national or international, and these letters sent to our members are no departure from that rule, for there are certain basic principles that transcend all partisanship; these are the prerogative of no party or nation, but are shared by all things living, because they are the laws of evolving life." In short, Fortune saw protecting her home against Hitler's potential invasion not as a political statement, but as an ethical one.

Engaging in a full-on psychic attack against Hitler is, perhaps, an extreme example of women using the occult to express a political stance, despite Fortune's protests to the contrary. Others have done it in quieter ways, though these ways have had lasting impacts that are still important today, as we'll discuss in later chapters. One thing is certain, however, and that is the availability of different forms of the occult to almost every woman. While men have been able to run for political office or enlist in the armed forces to fight wars at home and abroad, engaging in real action to support their political and social beliefs has not always been an option for women, who were often relegated to the realm of the home. A woman's sphere of influence was much smaller than it is now, so she had to find different avenues to exercise her power.

Fortune did live to see the end of Hitler's reign of terror. She died in 1946, while in England, and is buried in a cemetery in Glastonbury. Her tomb is still visited each year by hundreds of people, coming to pay their respects to a mystic whose philosophies still inspire many today.

"There are certain basic principles that transcend all partisanship; these are the prerogative of no party or nation, but are shared by all things living, because they are the laws of evolving life."

—Dion Fortune

WITCH

On Halloween 1968, Robin Morgan, Florika Remetier, Peggy Dobbins, Judy Duffett, Cynthia Funk, and Naomi Jaffe created a political activism group from hell. (Actually, it was from New York City, an offshoot of the New York Radical Women, the first women's liberation group in the Big Apple.) Initially, Morgan and company were more interested in what were called "zap actions," performative acts of protest intended to shock and unsettle people, as opposed to consciousness-raising events of persuasion. Eventually, the group would come to embrace a mix of the two methods, but their first action—simply naming their group—was a definite example of what the women came to refer to as "guerrilla theater," quick hit-and-run protests aimed at getting attention.

Welcome to the season of the WITCH, otherwise known as the Women's International Terrorist Conspiracy from Hell. For their inaugural march, the women took to the streets of New York to protest capitalism in complete witch garb. Wearing all black, with pointed hats and brooms, they protested—by hexing Wall Street, specifically targeting Chase Manhattan Bank. Apparently, it worked, as the market fell the next day. The movement grew from there.

In her 1970 anthology on the women's movement *Sisterhood Is*

Powerful, Robin Morgan remembered that "within a few weeks Covens had sprung up in such diverse spots as Boston, Chicago, San Francisco, North Carolina, Portland (Oregon), Austin (Texas), and Tokyo (Japan)." She went on to describe their lack of an overarching organization or leadership: "A certain common style—insouciance, theatricality, humor, and activism, unite the Covens—which are otherwise totally autonomous, and unhierarchical to the point of anarchy."

These groups of women organizing across the country were uniting under the WITCH manifesto, which read in part: "We are WITCH. We are LIBERATION. We are WE . . . WITCH means breaking the bonds of woman as a biologically and sexually defined creature. It implies the destruction of passivity, consumerism and commodity fetishism."

There was precedent for this occult angle in leftist organization, too. When Jerry Rubin and Abbie Hoffman, founders of the Youth International Party, were organizing protests against the Vietnam War, they decided they would get more attention if they staged a ritual exorcism of the Pentagon. And on October 21, 1967, they did. As women began separating from the larger leftist groups to dedicate themselves to pursuing feminism, different groups used different methods—such as witchcraft.

WITCH's Halloween hex worked so well in affecting the stock market that the group gathered again for another theatrical activism event, this time on Valentine's Day. The WITCHes descended (but not on brooms, of course) upon a bridal fair being held at Madison Square Garden. They took flight straight into the bridal fair, carrying signs that read "Confront the Whoremongers." Then, perhaps in a perversion of the Cinderella story, they let loose white mice. Needless to say, it didn't go over well, and WITCH's six-month reign of hexing in New York City ended. Other groups across the country, however, persisted.

The group's anarchist nature came through in the imaginative ways members adapted to their own specific situations and targets, often changing the meaning of the acronym WITCH to fit their purposes. When a group protested AT&T, they were Women Incensed at Telephone Company Harassment. At times, groups were Women's Independent Taxpayers, Consumers, and Homemakers or even Women Inspired to Commit Herstory. They kept conjuring new identities and methods.

Since then, WITCH may seem to have receded into our nation's past, but its influence on groups pursuing performative acts of protest is clear, especially in our current social-media-mobilized world of magical political resistance. And there have been flickers of a resurgence of the group during the political tumult of the past five to ten years. In 2019, Robin Morgan told *New York Times* reporter Jessica Bennett that she had been fielding questions from young protesters eager to take on the mission of WITCH. Given the group's lack of hierarchy and anonymous nature, clear information about a revival is sparse, but according to the *Chicagoist*, a group in Chicago using the name WITCH staged recent protests, including a 2016 protective spell to slow gentrification in Logan Square and a 2017 binding spell protest outside Trump Tower.

"WITCH lives and laughs in every woman. She is the free part of each of us, beneath the shy smiles, the acquiescence to absurd male domination, the make-up or flesh suffocating clothing our sick society demands."

—WITCH Manifesto

Joan Quigley

NANCY REAGAN'S SPIRITUAL ADVISOR

I f the 1960s and '70s were a time of protests for civil rights, then the '80s seemed to be a time to celebrate those hard-won rights, at least on the surface. The decade began by celebrating women as they stepped into their careers. Lily Tomlin, Jane Fonda, and Dolly Parton (the three muses, as far as we are concerned) fought misogyny and a mean boss in *9 to 5*, a film that embodied the "women can do it all" attitude that kicked off the 1980s. Even Barbie got in on the messaging. In 1984, Barbie Home and Office hit toy stores. The famous blonde doll donned a pink suit, complete with matching hat and briefcase, showing she was ready to tackle anything the business world had to throw at her. The playset let little girls everywhere play with Barbie sitting at her desk in her power suit. The tagline for the commercial was "We girls can do anything, right, Barbie?"

Of course, as women entered the workplace in unprecedented numbers, the fabric of society began to shift as well. There was economic prosperity, true, but there was also growing tension from the Cold War, fear (and a lot of miseducation) surrounding the AIDS epidemic, and the new reality that most households required two incomes to live comfortably. And since women were no longer at home, children were being left with babysitters or at daycare centers. In 1971, the National Organization for Women lobbied for affordable childcare options so that all women could have the opportunity to pursue work. Predictably, federally funded childcare never became a reality, as droves of conservatives opposed it. Still, women forged ahead.

At the same time that women were leaving the home for the workplace, various cultural fears surrounding the occult increased. These combined to create the beginnings of the Satanic Panic. One manifestation of this was related to the rising need for childcare and those poor little children who had to stay at the daycare while their mothers went to work. It wasn't long before rumors began to swirl that daycares and preschools were hotbeds for satanic activity. But it wasn't merely women entering the workforce that scared the public into seeing Satan around every corner.

Much of this moral panic stems from Michelle Proby's *Michelle Remembers* book, published in 1980 (more on that later), but the fear that satanic cults were waiting to sacrifice the innocent reached a fever pitch in the summer of 1983. A high-profile case in California led to the widespread fear—absurd, but still very genuine—that satanic cults were targeting young children for physical, sexual, and spiritual violence. These anxieties grew to the level of mass hysteria. And during the decade that made so many mothers scared for their children's souls, when some people saw the Devil in literally every detail, the president and his wife consulted the occult in their day-to-day lives.

That's right. Occultism had breached the walls of the White House, only Geraldo Rivera never did a special on it. This wasn't brand-new, of course. We've already met Madame Marcia, who advised Edith Wilson and Florence Harding, and even in her day the "red room" in the White House was already famous for the séances held there by Mary Todd Lincoln, wife of Abraham Lincoln. The Lincolns lost their son, Willie, to typhoid fever at age eleven, and

Mary Todd turned to mediums to try to speak to him. Jane Pierce, wife of President Franklin Pierce, also used mediums to contact the dead during her time in the White House.

But no other administration had quite the relationship to the occult enjoyed by the Reagan administration. While the Satanic Panic raged on, President and First Lady Reagan quietly consulted their own occult advisor.

Marlin Fitzwater, White House press secretary during the Reagan administration, confirmed to the *New York Times* in May 1988 that Nancy Reagan did consult an astrologer, especially after the stress of her husband's attempted assassination in 1981, but Fitzwater assured the public that "no policy or decision in my mind has ever been influenced by astrology."

There are many who dispute this. Donald Regan, who served as White House chief of staff during the Reagan years, wrote in his memoir, "Virtually every major move and decision the Reagans made during my time as White House chief of staff was cleared in advance with a woman in San Francisco who drew up horoscopes to make certain that the planets were in favorable alignment for the enterprise." That woman was Joan Quigley, astrologer to Nancy Reagan. Quigley wrote a memoir about her relationship with the Reagans, which the *New York Times* blasted in a review, calling the book "perfectly dreadful—the writing is ghastly, the book is repetitive, poorly organized, badly edited, silly and shallow. It's also fascinating, in a bizarre, morbid and bitchy way." Ouch. Nancy Reagan was also publicly mocked for her belief in astrology (the First Lady apparently would beg Quigley not to talk to the press about their relationship).

So just how involved was Quigley in daily affairs of the White House? According to her memoir, she consulted astrological charts before any major events on the Reagans' calendar. She suggested the best times for Air Force One to take off, for the State of the Union address to be scheduled, and for meetings to be held with foreign leaders like Mikhail Gorbachev. Donald Regan organized the president's calendar with color-coded notes indicating "good" days and "bad" days when scheduling the events for the Reagans. Regan reportedly didn't get along with the First Lady at all, and this kind of micromanagement from her astrologer apparently did not help their relationship.

Quigley even helped Nancy Reagan cultivate the perfect image for a First Lady, completely overhauling how the public perceived her. In an interview with the *Hollywood Reporter*, Quigley's sister Ruth detailed how Quigley molded the First Lady:

> *Nancy listened religiously to what Joan had to say. Joan was the first one who changed Nancy's image. You might remember there was a recession when Reagan first took over after the Carter years. And so Nancy bought China [dishes] for the White House—which is hardly extravagant; after all the White House is where the nation entertains for state dinners. I think Nancy thought she'd be another Jackie Kennedy because she was a lady with style and liked to dress well. But this was an era that wasn't very accepting of that, and she was criticized in the press. Joan helped her turn her image around. [. . .] She told Nancy to do some volunteer work, to stay out of the fashion magazines. And Nancy followed that.*

On the one hand, Quigley appeared to have enormous control over what was happening in the White House. After all, according to what Regan said, Nancy Reagan was not the only one who listened to Quigley's astrological predictions—everyone knew the good and bad days to schedule events. In a sense, Quigley was in charge of scheduling at the White House. That someone outside the White House had that much control over American politics is shocking—and worthy of more scrutiny than this relationship has gotten. On the other hand, Nancy Reagan's reliance on her relationship to Quigley, in light of the attempt on the president's life, can be seen sympathetically. Nancy Reagan was in a vulnerable position, and it is completely understandable that she would lean toward whatever stability she could.

Of course, all of this gains a new level of relevance when viewed today, in the context of Donald Trump. If there was one thing Trump enjoyed doing during his presidential campaign, it was comparing himself to President Reagan, partially to feed the image that the GOP upholds evangelical Christian conservative values. This comparison is clearly part of a carefully curated public image (holding upside-down Bibles, mispronouncing New Testament books, and all). There may not be much religion behind the scenes, but voters want to see a religious lifestyle.

Perhaps this explains why Nancy Reagan was so adamant about hiding her relationship to a woman like Joan Quigley. Quigley may have told the First Lady when and where to go, but Nancy Reagan couldn't tarnish her pristine public image.

The Devil's Advocates

n 2021, Texas passed a law that outlawed abortions after six weeks. Many were outraged, arguing that many women don't even know they are pregnant until after the six-week mark. Another worrisome aspect of the law: it encouraged Texans to both monitor and turn in their neighbors who either got an abortion or assisted someone in getting an abortion.

Enter the Satanic Temple, an occult activist organization that pushes for religious and reproductive rights. Formed in 2012, the Satanic Temple (which is distinct from the older, more self-indulgent Church of Satan founded in 1966 by Anton LaVey) doesn't encourage the worship of the Devil or any demons; rather, it seeks to promote ethics and individuality within secular humanism. The temple's mission, according to its website, is to fight for equality; thus, it is more an advocacy group than a religious organization. Current and past campaigns have included installing a statue of Baphomet at the Arkansas state capitol as a statement on religious iconography in public buildings;

forming "After School Satan Clubs" to combat evangelical groups promoting themselves as aftercare programs in public schools; and performing a "pink mass" at the gravesite of Fred Phelps, the founder of the controversial Westboro Baptist Church (the group that picketed graves of bombing victims to spread their hate speech against the LGBTQ community). In the twenty-first century, "Hail Satan" means less signing the Devil's book in blood and more fighting for equal rights and against hate.

Reproductive rights are an explicit part of the Satanic Temple's tenets—one of its core beliefs is that "one's body is inviolable, subject to one's own will alone"—so after the Texas law was passed, the temple used its tax-exempt IRS status as a legally recognized church to intervene on the behalf of Texan women. The group developed an "abortion ritual" that it said would classify first-trimester abortions as a religious right; interfering with a pregnant temple member's ability to perform this ritual is tantamount to religious persecution. According to the Religious Freedom Restoration Act of 1993, the government cannot interfere in a religious activity, as freedom of religious worship is a protected freedom. (This act was originally passed to allow for the use of peyote in some Native American religions.) By invoking this act and its legal standing as a federally recognized church, the Satanic Temple is actively fighting the Texas abortion law and helping women obtain safe and legal

The Witches Who Hexed Trump

MAGICAL RESISTANCE

We are living in a golden age of online witchery. Pinterest offers aesthetics and spells for every kind of witch: baby witches, cottage witches, hearth witches, kitchen witches, sea witches, forest witches, city witches, tech witches. There are ready-made Instagrammable graphics explaining what candle colors correspond to each spell. There are entire websites devoted to the uses of herbs and, of course, crystals. A quick Google search offers thousands of definitions for paganism, Wicca, and witchcraft, which are all different paths. Tarot readings on YouTube (often called "Pick a Card"s) will garner thousands, if not millions, of views.

Over on YouTube, witches have channels with names like "The Witch of Wonderlust" (over 300,000 subscribers), "The Green Witch" (over 200,000 subscribers), and "Mintfaery" (over 120,000 subscribers). Anyone wishing to get tips to start their witchcraft journey can simply click a video and get going. Witches are also going strong on Tumblr; the hashtags #witch and #wicca have more than 75,000 followers, and #magick has a whopping 306,000, with tips on spells, altars, and circle casting.

Probably the biggest boon for witchcraft has been WitchTok—the witchy side of the video-sharing platform TikTok. The social media site may be the most popular platform for young witches and those interested in the occult. In an interview with *Nylon*, one user, Caitlyn/Kalliope (she's on TikTok as @okaries, with nearly 400,000 followers) explained the popularity of the app: "TikTok is a much more personal thing than YouTube, Twitter, Instagram, or anything like that, because you can directly talk to your fans." That intimacy, she said, is behind the popularity of WitchTok, which lets young practitioners feel that they're in a coven of hundreds of thousands. Unlike YouTube, which is more about offering tarot readings or giving tips for spellwork, or Instagram, which features individual witches and their practices, TikTok offers a platform for community. WitchTok has instructions for spells and general information for the baby witches of the internet, but it is also a place for people to post videos asking for help, or guidance, or advice as they embark on their journey. It's a place where witches can be "out" and proud of their craft too, especially if they are living in homes or towns that don't support that journey. Would-be occult participants can learn the ins and outs of spell work, hexes, tarot, and astrology—there's even information on goddess worship and how to work with your chosen goddess. It's a safe space to grow, and the community is welcoming, for the most part.

Instagram seems like it was custom-made for the current witchcraft boom. Influencers are already creating perfect aesthetics for their picture-perfect feed, and witchy influencers do not disappoint, with their glam goth looks, all long black dresses and oversized chic black pointy witch hats. The #witchesofinstagram hashtag has over seven million posts, most posed pictures of pretty women (and people of all genders) with flawless makeup and manicured nails. The long nails are showing off pastel and glittery crystals. Some posts show lit candles of all colors (though red and white seem to be the most popular); some show elaborate tarot card spreads on plush backgrounds. It's an aspirational lifestyle, occult-style.

But it would be a mistake to think that online witches are all doing it just for the 'gram. WitchTok, witch Tumblr (Witchblr), and Witchstagram can also be potent spaces for social and political activism. Occult activism is booming, with trending topics like #witchesforblm and #witchesforbiden. Search #pagan, and you'll find that the topic has 1.8 billion views. And of course, there was the movement to hex Donald Trump.

In 2016, after a contentious and drama-filled campaign, Donald Trump became president of the United States. The previous year of political scandals and grandstanding had been marked by misogyny; Trump was running against Hillary Clinton, the first female presidential candidate backed by a major party, so naturally, she was called a demon, a hag, and an assortment of other insults, all aiming to cast her as an evil woman by using occult-related language. She even weathered Satanic Panic–style accusations that she was sacrificing children to use their blood in satanic rituals, or running a child-sex-trafficking ring out of a pizzeria's basement. On the other side, one of the many horrors of the 2016 campaign came in October when the media released video of Trump in 2005 proclaiming to TV personality Billy Bush that he could "grab [women] by the pussy" because he was a rich and famous man. It was patriarchal and class privilege at their worst.

By 2017, witches were trending on social media, with the hashtag #magicalresistance connecting thousands of activists across the country in their stance against the president. These self-identified witches emerged in full force, placing hexes and binding spells on Trump to block him from using his power to harm himself or others. In February 2017, the BBC reported that thousands of American witches were organizing on a Facebook page, planning a midnight hex on the new president. The participants interviewed said this was less about harming Trump and more about stopping him from causing harm. Elsewhere on the web, internet witches shared spells on TikTok involving yellow-toupeed effigy dolls or short orange candles (substitute a Cheeto, if needed, some recommended). Even singer Lana Del Rey urged her fans to join her in casting a spell to stop Trump from causing chaos. Nor did the online witches stop with Trump. They also came together in droves to protect women by targeting men accused of predatory behavior like Brock Turner, the Stanford student who served only months of his sentence after sexually assaulting a woman, and Brett Kavanaugh, the Supreme Court nominee, and now judge, who defended himself against allegations of assault in front of the nation.

The magical resistance against political figures like Trump wasn't new in 2017. It was an evolution of an old idea from the feminist messages of nineteenth-century séances to magical attempts to use spells to protect England from the Nazis in World War II to the shocking protests of WITCH in the 1960s and 1970s. Accusations of occult behavior or witchcraft have been lobbed at women who didn't fit into society, flung at them as an insult, but the occult and witchcraft have simultaneously been used by women to grab power when it was withheld from them and to protest the status quo. Society may try to isolate and ostracize women with accusations of witchcraft or evil, but witches can join together and fight back, and they have.

Most people think of witches as fairy-tale villains, or perhaps part of our early colonial history. They're staples of folklore and often make appearances in horror movies. But today's occult women— these witches on social media protesting misogyny—are political activists. They are not living a fictional stereotype of witches as

Women have only made up a small sliver of our country's long political history. Part of that is because the idea of female ambition is still considered a rather nasty idea to many (see Hillary Clinton's bid for the presidency and the moral panic that ensued). Women, therefore, have had to get creative if they wanted a seat at the White House. Victoria Woodhull, the first woman to run for president, was a psychic medium, using her platform and audience to bolster her campaign. Other women, like Madame Marcia and Joan Quigley, took a kind of back door, choosing not to run themselves, but rather to seek an advisory position to presidents and First Ladies. Others took the route of opposition, using the occult as a direct confrontation to power, as with the WITCH movement and the political hexes during the Trump administration.

Once an astrologer can be "at the hub of power" in the White House, the doors open to much more. The occult offered women ways to support themselves outside of the home and several practitioners even created lucrative careers. Many even became famous, entrancing the public with the paranormal possibilities of communication with an afterlife.

3

GHOSTS
AND
GLORY

MONETIZING THE OCCULT

In the mid-nineteenth century, women—or, at least, proper women—were expected to be at home. They were wives and mothers, or else they assisted those women in the home as hired help. And because of the culture's insistence that women stay in the home, women were also seen as nurturers and caretakers. Leadership roles of any kind were off-limits for women, including in religion. While women could instruct their children in religious matters, they could not be ministers or priests. The occult offered women the opportunity to gain a voice in the public sphere of traditional religion. Women like Marie Laveau and Achsa Sprague made room for themselves in male-dominated religions. Others, like Madame Blavatsky, Alice Bailey, and Edna Ballard, used the occult not only to gain leadership positions but also as a platform to create their own spiritual communities and to espouse new philosophical ideas.

Of course, this was nothing new. Women had been steadily rising to more prominent religious roles since Spiritualism began gaining national traction in the nineteenth century. The Spiritualist movement, in which spirit mediums (most of them women) acted as translators or conduits for messages from the other side, gave proper ladies a way of surviving and even financially thriving under these constraints. The Fox sisters, with their enormous public success, proved that Spiritualism could make a woman famous. Two of the women who followed Maggie and Kate Fox down the path to notoriety were Mina Crandon and Leonora Piper. Crandon, called the "witch of Lime Street" by her biographer David Jaher, was a physical medium who performed in her own home for friends and family, never charging money. She became a popular name in the media of the early 1920s because of her participation in the *Scientific American* contest to find an authentic psychic practitioner. She was investigated by a committee composed of scientists, psychic investigators, and magicians in order to see if her manifestations were real. Her open conflict with Harry Houdini, who believed she was a fraud, became popular fodder for newspapers of the time. Like Crandon, trance medium Leonora Piper did not take money for sittings and also found herself involved in investigations of her psychic potential. While Crandon faced Houdini and the media, Piper faced William James and the American Society for Psychical Research and later the psychologists Amy E. Tanner and G. Stanley Hall. Several members of the Society for Psychical Research acknowledged her abilities, which made her a well-known medium of her time.

While many mediums were like Crandon and Piper, working out of their homes for little to no money, some saw an opportunity to turn these psychic investigations into a career for themselves. The business of being a psychic offered a lucrative path for women who couldn't find a future elsewhere. It was a money-making opportunity—and one that allowed women a kind of freedom that hadn't been offered to them previously. If women were told by society to stay at home, then stay at home they would. Like every good 1950s Tupperware saleswoman, they turned the home's parlor and living room into a place to make a good living. And there was money to be made, there's no doubt about that. Once communication with the dead became big business, it remained that way. By the 1990s, television psychics and mediums took over the airwaves. Following the 9/11 attacks in 2001, perhaps as a result of the ensuing period of loss and uncertainty, the TV landscape was flooded with shows about psychic mediums, all of whom claimed to speak to people's dead relatives and offer comfort in a time of grief.

In the early to mid-twentieth century, women were using the broad world of the occult as a way to enter the entrepreneurial world, which wasn't often open to women. In the 1920s and '30s, Evangeline

Adams built an empire from her astrology business, running a successful New York City business catering to the elite of the city, while also hosting an immensely popular nationwide radio show. Adams was one of the first women to run astrological predictions in newspapers, but she also marks a more important milestone in the history of women and the occult. The business world was (and still is, to some degree) considered the realm of men, but the occult world belonged to women. Adams successfully bridged those two, becoming one of the country's top businesswomen in her day.

Like Adams, there's a long history of women who have used the media to espouse their own occult ideas. Author Margaret St. Clair, while not a practitioner of astrology as Adams was, still used her vast knowledge of Wicca to craft her horror and science fiction stories in the mid-twentieth century. She added Wiccan rituals and symbols to her fiction to show how pagan religion could play a role in the lives of ordinary characters. By the latter half of the century and into the new millennium, women like Lorraine Warren, Miss Cleo, and Stormy Daniels were using their psychic skills to gain fame through television, film, and the internet. Warren began her journey to fame as a clairvoyant working with her husband, Ed Warren (a self-proclaimed demonologist), investigating popular cases of hauntings and possessions. Some of their more infamous investigations include the Amityville house and the Enfield poltergeist in the United Kingdom. The Warrens ran a museum for decades, showing off haunted objects collected over the years. Though their credibility has been challenged numerous times, Lorraine Warren became a darling of the paranormal investigation show circuit on television in the early 2000s.

Miss Cleo was one of the most recognizable television psychics, thanks to late-night commercials for the Psychic Readers Network, which ran from 1997 to 2003. Unlike the Warrens, Miss Cleo never sought more glory after her stint as the spokeswoman for the network, though she did continue her career as a psychic, publishing a book on the subject matter, perhaps proving that the occult spotlight can offer a platform for crafting one's public persona. Stormy Daniels hasn't yet reached the popularity of Miss Cleo—at least not for her psychic abilities—though she has turned to the world of occult shows to help change the public opinion of her. Following her affair with Donald Trump (which came to light during his presidential campaign), Daniels took her own psychic investigation show, *Spooky Babes*, on the road, showing that the occult may provide a ready-made platform for reinvention.

The women in this chapter are wildly different from one another. Some sought the occult for religious enlightenment, while others saw dollar signs. Whatever their motive, they manipulated the occult space for their own benefit, gaining fame—and sometimes infamy.

Marie Laveau

THE BUSINESS OF VOODOO

American pop culture has often been very white in its portrayals of the occult, unless you count all the magical Black women that white authors and screenwriters love to lean on in their fiction. Historically, mediums of color, especially as they are portrayed in fiction, haven't had the easiest time finding mainstream success (they are either mythologized or relegated to the "magical Black woman" trope), but portrayals have been diversifying in recent years. One notable example is Angela Bassett's Marie Laveau in *American Horror Story: Coven*, which of course depicts a real (and highly influential) occult practitioner from history.

Laveau is known as the "voodoo queen of New Orleans." Every year droves of tourists flock to what is considered to be her tomb in St. Louis Cemetery No. 1. She even somehow became part of the Marvel Comics universe. But Laveau's life has sometimes been obscured by the legends surrounding her legacy.

Laveau was born in 1801 as a free woman of color to Marguerite D'Arcantel and Charles Leveaux (though some claim her father was a wealthy slave-owning plantation owner). She was considered a "quadroon," or a person of one-quarter African descent, which put her in the middle of a complicated ranking system in antebellum New Orleans society. In other words, she enjoyed more social mobility than someone who was considered "fully" Black.

Though she was raised Roman Catholic (baptized as a newborn and married in New Orleans's famous St. Louis Cathedral), she is best known for her voodoo practices, which she built into a web of influence that spanned the city. New Orleans voodoo is a spiritual and cultural practice of the American Black diaspora, derived from West African religions and the Haitian religion of Vodou, which involves working with spirits and deities. Spirit possession is an important Vodou ritual. But Laveau began her career not as a psychic or voodoo priestess, but as a hairdresser. This role brought her family money and gave Laveau access to the wealthy families of New Orleans. As she styled and cut the hair of her Black clientele, she learned the secrets of the wealthier families for which those clients worked.

This may have been the start of her new occult career, but Laveau's legend as a voodoo priestess began when she married Jacques Paris in 1819. Paris disappeared under mysterious circumstances only a year later—and rumors began circulating that Laveau used powerful magic to get rid of her first husband. In 1821, she flouted social expectations and marriage laws forbidding interracial relationships when she moved in with Captain Christophe Glapion, a son of an aristocratic family, with whom she would have five children.

Though Glapion's aristocratic lineage may have suggested that Laveau was enjoying a life of wealth and luxury, the public records of the time suggest otherwise. Apparently, Glapion was in a lot of debt at the time of his death. Laveau couldn't read or write, but her advice was sought by the wealthy upper crust of New Orleans society. And this was where she thrived.

Using her access to the elite of the city through her hairdressing business, Laveau began to offer her voodoo cures for everything from healing the sick to securing love to helping women conceive. Her family reportedly had connections to different lineages of African spiritual practices, but Laveau herself became a student under Dr. John Bayou, a Senegalese root worker who was well-known in the New Orleans area. Doctor John, as he was known, was a freed Black man who taught Laveau the art of gris-gris, a practice of amulet magic that can provide everything from luck to birth control. He also introduced Laveau to voodoo society in New Orleans, which had its own ranking system and meetings. Laveau quickly became a queen within voodoo society, leading ceremonies and gatherings.

Her cottage on St. Ann Street, owned by Glapion, was the hub for her practice, which included root magic, ceremonies, and rituals, sometimes including conjuring the spirit of the Great Zombi, a figure from Haitian folklore. She used her magic practices to help during the yellow fever outbreaks that plagued the city more than once. She also offered nonmagical gatherings for Black New Orleans residents in her home, making it a place for people to connect and work through their collective trauma in the slave-owning culture of the South.

But it is important to note that Laveau did not invent the voodoo tradition in New Orleans, even though it is her name that most people know today. Women like Sanité Dédé and Marie Saloppé practiced voodoo and root magic to help New Orleanians through their troubles, both in the home (lots of troubled relationships and financial problems) and in the greater city (floods and epidemics were common complaints).

Through her voodoo work, Laveau cared for the residents of New Orleans, raising at least ten adopted children and working with the sick during the yellow fever epidemics. She also raised funds for churches in the area. She passed away on June 15, 1881, and is rumored to be buried in the Glapion tomb in New Orleans's St. Louis Cemetery No. 1 in the French Quarter. Today, tourists flock to her presumed gravesite to pay homage to the most famous voodoo priestess in New Orleans.

Achsa Sprague

HEALED BY SPIRITS

n a religious culture that actively impeded women's access to education and to a voice in society, Spiritualism offered women a unique position that they had never had in the American landscape. They were able to make money while keeping their "angel in the house" image intact. In 1849, Achsa W. Sprague, a teacher from Plymouth Notch, Vermont, was twenty years old when she became bedridden from a disease that attacked her joints, most likely rheumatoid arthritis. Prior to falling ill, Sprague lived an independent life. She had taught school since she was twelve years old. It was not only a job that she was good at, but also her sole source of income. More than that, she financially supported her family with her earnings.

At first, Sprague refused to let her illness change her habits. A bit of a stubborn rebel, she refused to give up on her career or her life. When she found that her illness had made it difficult for her to walk to school, Sprague began riding a horse, which she found she enjoyed. Soon, though, even that proved difficult due to pain. In one of her lowest points, she was confined to a bed in her mother's house. The loss of independence was for Sprague much worse than any physical pain. Doctors came and went. No one seemed to know how to heal her body enough to give Sprague her old life back.

Her disease, which had progressively gotten worse over the past five years, had taken away her job prospects—that is, until a miracle occurred. While in bed, Sprague had a habit of communing with the spirits, and one day, those same spirits healed her. Within the year and with the regained use of her limbs, she took to the road, appearing as a public medium and a speaker on the subject of Spiritualism.

Sprague's story seems to be a basic one, at least in Spiritualism: a young woman talks to spirits and spins it into a successful career. In fact, she seems to share more than a little in common with the Fox sisters. But Sprague's illness makes her story unique. Actually, it is her response to her illness—and how it sets her against traditional religion—that makes her story stand out.

Sprague grew up poor. From an early age, she was a breadwinner for her family, which gave her more autonomy than most of her peers. She had students who looked up to her and she had enough money to have some social mobility in her town. Then she became disabled by her illness. She couldn't walk, which soon meant she couldn't teach. Sprague went from being an independent woman in every sense of the word to being confined to a bed in her mother's house. Spiritualism let her overcome societal barriers to women's success, as it did for many other young mediums. But it also seemed to help her find relief from the illness that was making it physically impossible for her to work or live independently.

Following her healing by the spirits, Sprague wrote and lectured about how the spirits healed her body and spirit. Using literary license (referring to her spirit guide as an angel), she wrote a poem in her diary called "The Angel's Visit" in which she describes her room as "a living tomb" and her body as a "neglected lute, with broken strings all sadly mute"—until the angel tunes each string and brings music through her once again. An angel heals a body and that is something to be celebrated, in Sprague's eyes. In her later lectures (and the public trances she would often speak in), Sprague was positively evangelical about her newfound Spiritualist beliefs.

Why is this significant? How is this different from anyone who believes that God—or another deity, for that matter—has healed them from an illness? The Puritanical Christian faith in which Sprague was well-versed welcomed suffering. After all, lowly humans are here on earth to suffer because of their sins, until they reap eternal reward in heaven. This tradition thus suggests that suffering is something to be celebrated. Sprague defiantly rejected that. Spiritualism allowed her a space to say that she deserved health—and wealth. She wasn't born sinful or unworthy. Her human vessel was ready-made for the divine, no changes needed.

Once she began her career as a Spiritualist lecturer, Sprague was in high demand, traveling across the country. After an appearance in Terre Haute, Indiana, one man described her this way: "Miss Sprague is our criterion as to all that is good, great, eloquent and beautiful." In Troy, New York, another said this: "The more I talk with the members of *Our Church* the stronger is my conviction that you are the only one that can give full satisfaction in our pulpit." She would sometimes get close to one hundred requests a year to speak at Spiritualist churches and conventions. Quite an impressive résumé for a woman who once felt as if her body was rebelling against her.

"Mediums were known for their receptivity, an ostensibly feminine trait. Thus female mediums were able to have their voices heard in public by speaking, not as themselves, but as others."

—Dr. Erin Forbes, "Do Black Ghosts Matter? Harriet Jacobs' Spiritualism"

Mina "Margery" Crandon

THE WITCH OF LIME STREET

I n 1922, research into occult phenomena moved beyond the realm of clubs and societies and went mainstream. And the press loved it. The owner of *Scientific American*, Orson Munn, announced that his magazine was instituting a prize for a verified psychic who could produce physical effects, such as table tilting, teleportation, and the creation of ectoplasm. The purpose of the prize was not necessarily to prove the existence of an afterlife or spirit communication, but rather to document a psychic who could truly manifest phenomena that science could not explain.

The committee of experts, who would evaluate the psychics and verify who was the real deal, was made up of five men: Dr. Walter Franklin Prince of the American Society for Psychical Research (ASPR); Dr. William McDougall, an eminent Harvard psychologist and president of the ASPR; Dr. Daniel Frost Comstock, a former professor at MIT and the inventor of Technicolor, who specialized in physics and engineering; Dr. Hereward Carrington, author and researcher for the ASPR; and Harry Houdini, the master magician, escape artist, and illusionist. Malcolm Bird, an editor of the magazine, was the wrangler of the contest and committee, though he later fell into dispute with certain members, in particular Houdini, and was taken off the project.

The prize totaled $5,000: $2,500 for a psychic who could produce physical effects, and $2,500 for an authentic spirit photographer. It was a lot of money for the time, equivalent to more than $80,000 today. Winning this prize also would offer the prestige of legitimacy conferred by scientists. The organizers and fierce proponents of Spiritualism, like Arthur Conan Doyle, thought mediums would be lining up around the block to be proven authentic.

Instead, except for a few easily dismissed volunteers, there were crickets.

Since so few volunteered, Doyle had to get creative. He had recently met an American medium in England, which is how Mina, or "Margery" (her alias to protect her from the press), Crandon of Lime Street in Beacon Hill, Boston, was recommended to the committee. Crandon was ultimately chosen for investigation for various reasons. For one, she lived in Beacon Hill with her husband, Dr. Le Roi Goddard Crandon, a Harvard-trained doctor and surgeon. Her upper-class position, even if she rose to it from rural roots and a first marriage to the owner of a grocery store, was secure. She didn't take pay for her sittings, and she was shy with the press. Her husband, a recent convert to Spiritualism, pushed her to perform for experts once she showed psychic gifts, but she seemed to see sittings as something entertaining that she did with their close circle of friends. The committee was pleased that she wasn't seeking fame; they thought that it might imply her talents were real. By their line of reasoning, she was less likely to be a fraud if she wasn't performing for money.

Crandon had developed an interest in mediumship early in 1923, the same year she came under investigation. She and a close friend had decided to visit a medium, though Crandon claimed she was not a believer and went for fun. During the sitting, the medium relayed messages to her from her deceased brother, Walter. Walter was five years older than Crandon, and he died in a gruesome railroad accident in 1911 when he was twenty-eight years old. The two had been very close. Walter dabbled in spirit communication when he was young, and his primary message to her during her sitting was that she was sensitive and should take up "The Work."

Crandon didn't believe this message initially, but soon after her reading, her husband decided to run experiments among their close friends to see who may have had psychic abilities without knowing it. He invited a small group over one evening and gathered them in a room after dinner to attempt a séance. During this test run, while the Crandons and their friends held hands around a table in the dimly lit room, the table vibrated strongly and tipped over. One at a time, the participants left the room to see if the table would stop shaking. It stopped when Mina Crandon left the room.

After this, Crandon's life became a string of nightly séances and performances, at first only for their friends. Her husband took her on a tour abroad, and she was tested by Dr. Charles-Robert Richet in Paris and met Doyle in London. These contacts brought her to the attention of the people in charge of the *Scientific American* contest.

Beyond her class status and her lack of interest in profit, she was a prime candidate for one more reason: her effects were prolific, sensational, and broadly rowdy. Her spirit control was her brother, Walter, and he was everything that Crandon, as an upper-class woman, was not supposed to be. He was crass, vulgar, funny, antagonistic, at times violent, and yet entertaining and charming. Music would play on the Victrola the whole time, sometimes slowing and sometimes speeding up. The table would do more than shake and tilt; it would turn over, and supposedly, it occasionally pushed people through different rooms of the house. She went into trances and delivered messages. Objects flew through the air or were teleported, at times through walls, according to sitters. And she performed in low red light so the ectoplasm she produced would show up to best effect. Ectoplasm was a jelly-like substance thought to be created by spirit contact. The stuff would ooze from the body cavities of mediums, including from the nose, the mouth, ears, and other more private areas. Sometimes, it would form appendages and touch sitters or have an image attached. Crandon's ectoplasm came most often from her lap.

The committee tried to prove that Crandon's psychic abilities were real by attempting to rule out all potential methods of fraud— for instance, they immobilized her hands and feet so that she couldn't secretly move objects and say a spirit did it. Crandon was able to circumvent most of the preventative measures, until Houdini joined the test séances. Houdini became personally obsessed with defeating her, seemingly fearing that confirmation by the committee, coupled with her preexisting popularity, would make the public believe communication with the dead was possible. He constructed a tight-fitting cabinet that kept only Crandon's head and extremities exposed, and he made sure her husband wasn't in his usual spot at her right side. With this new innovation, Crandon's performance was hampered. Houdini's box worked.

Crandon had other weaknesses, short of being put fully inside a box. She insisted that her husband hold at least one of her hands during the séances. When he was replaced with an investigator, the spirits didn't react as they usually did, leading to speculation that her husband helped in her performance, or at least wasn't as restrictive of her movements as an outsider might be. During the last couple of years of Houdini's life, he specifically singled out Crandon's techniques for exposure in his shows. In a 1925 show in Boston's Symphony Hall, he performed an exposé of many of her "tricks" by replicating them, if he could, and explaining how he believed she achieved her effects. According to Houdini and Crandon biographer David Jaher, he went so far as to make a message from Walter appear on a slate, along with a copy of a photograph of Walter at the moment of his grisly and violent death—a picture of her brother Crandon had never seen and did not know about. On the Spiritualists' side, Walter (via Crandon, of course) and various mediums across the country rooted for Houdini's failure and even his death, which came in October 1926.

The *Scientific American* prize committee members ultimately voted no on Crandon, but she still had some proponents on the committee who believed she was the real deal and argued in her favor. In 1925, a year after the *Scientific American* investigation, her deceptions were fully exposed by a group of Harvard graduate students and professors in the sciences and the humanities. Her ectoplasm had already been debunked earlier in the year as being made up of animal organs and tracheas sewn into other shapes. But the later study showed how she was able to circumvent control by sitters who held her hands: using her feet to move and throw objects and touch people. Her flexibility and agility helped her to take advantage of any bit of wiggle room she had. And the low lighting confused sitters.

Why Houdini focused so much on Crandon is still an open question, though. While she was gaining publicity and maybe swaying the public's belief, she wasn't making money from her sittings. She didn't charge for readings. Interestingly, Houdini repeatedly emphasized that she used her feminine wiles of seduction to distract investigators and win them to her side. As he would do in the fortune-telling hearings of 1926, he focused on sexual impropriety as the sin of mediums. Jaher points out a telling contradiction in Houdini's own characterizations of Crandon and her supporters. While he denied any kind of supernatural power existed and claimed that Crandon was a fraud, he still used terminology related to voodoo, black magic, and witchcraft to describe her slipperiness. For her part, in an interview Crandon compared herself to an accused witch in Salem of the 1600s, only she said she had to face panels of scientists instead of judges.

LAW AND ORDER: PSYCHIC DIVISION

n pop culture as well as in life, women have sometimes been able to sidle into positions of power—like police detective—via the occult. Not everyone in the spooky detective category is a woman (what's up, Agent Cooper from *Twin Peaks*), but on television as well as off, we see a gendered breakdown of investigative modes.

Take *The Dead Files*, a television show that premiered in 2011 and starred Amy Allan and Steve DiShiavi as the main team of investigators. Here, we have a man and a woman working together, both taking a lead role (unlike earlier shows, like *Ghost Hunters*, where the women were clearly the junior members of the team). But in this show, she is the psychic and he is the "science/hard facts" of it all. Over the course of the show, Amy uses her psychic talents to channel the dead, often walking around wide-eyed on-screen as she experiences what the ghost wants her to feel or see or hear. Steve, though, isn't given to this kind of paranormal performance. He's a retired homicide detective (from the NYPD, no less), and as such, his role is to do the research on the haunted site, by talking to historians and local citizens. He's cerebral, logical. She's the emotional connection.

The show, to its credit, doesn't seem to favor Amy over Steve, or vice versa. Rather, they work together to figure out exactly what (or more precisely, who) is haunting the location. Still, it is troubling to see that, for the most part, these shows are still following the model of the gendered occult. Women are still wandering around homes talking to spirits, while the men are the logical investigators looking to science for answers.

Medium, which starred Patricia Arquette, was an interesting variation on this theme. In that show, the "psychic investigator" was also a woman—but she *directly* reflected real-life professional psychics, because the show was based on the memoirs of Allison DuBois, who claimed to work as a "profiler" consultant to law-enforcement agencies, channeling both living criminals and dead victims to crack difficult cases. (The agencies in question disagree that she assisted them.) *Medium* and the similar show *Ghost Whisperer*, based on the work of television psychic Mary Ann Winkowski, started airing in the mid-2000s alongside another show featuring a police consultant who boasts of supernatural powers. *Psych* focuses on Shawn Spencer, played by James Roday, who works as a psychic detective—but in the world of the show he's not actually psychic, instead perpetrating a long-term fraud where he uses his superior skills of observation and analysis to solve crimes. Even with a male occult investigator, *Psych* still reinforces the trope of masculine logic and reason. *The X-Files* is a notable exception to this, but we will discuss Agents Mulder and Scully later.

Madame Helena Blavatsky

GURU OF A PSYCHIC RELIGION

Madame Blavatsky was born Helena Petrovna von Hahn on August 12, 1831, in Russia, to Helena de Fadeyev (a novelist who was called the "George Sand of Russia") and Colonel Peter von Hahn. Her story begins just as dramatically as one would expect from a girl who would become an occult celebrity: with a teenage mother and an absent father in the midst of a cholera epidemic. Both newborn Blavatsky and her mother were so ill that last rites were administered. Even that ritual was dramatic, as the priest accidentally set his own robes on fire during the rite. Despite everything, both the infant Blavatsky and her mother survived.

Her father was gone through much of her childhood, stationed in Poland, and her parents separated briefly. During that time, Blavatsky traveled with her mother. This marked the first time she was exposed to Tibetan Buddhism, something that would shape her later in life. Her parents did eventually reconcile, but Blavatsky's life was once again upended when her mother contracted tuberculosis, which eventually took her life. Before she died, her mother brought Blavatsky to her side and told her that she was a remarkable child, who was not like others. Blavatsky apparently took her mother's words to heart, as she grew into a woman who many believed was one of a kind.

Young Blavatsky spent much of her childhood with her grandparents, especially her grandmother, Princess Dolgorukov, an educated woman who was descended from royalty. Blavatsky was raised rather differently from daughters of other aristocratic families; she was allowed to read widely and, like her grandmother, was highly educated. She also was able to spend a lot of her time in the royal library, where she read books on occult knowledge and other mystical subjects. These esoteric subjects fascinated her, as did anything having to do with the paranormal. As a child in her grandparents' home, Blavatsky had sleep problems, and there are family stories about how Blavatsky wouldn't play with other children—but she did play with the ghosts that haunted the home.

Her origin story as a remarkable occult figure began around this time too. She fell from a horse and said that a mysterious (and perhaps ghostly) man saved her. She called him her "protector" and described him as a man from India. More and more frequently, she said she dreamed of the man. She also began to describe a life beyond this physical one, a life she claimed to live on the astral plane. It was a lot of unusual talk from a teenage girl who was expected to marry into an aristocratic family.

As an adult, she married Nikifor Vladimirovich Blavatsky, a vice governor of a Russian province. Her parents wished her to marry a well-matched man, someone who was wealthy and high in station. Even though she initially consented to the union, Blavatsky frequently ran away. Perhaps her new husband should've seen that one coming: Blavatsky, in her marriage vows, refused to say the word *obey*. In the 1850s, she began her travels, first to Paris, then London, and finally on to the United States, inspired by the writings of James Fenimore Cooper. There, Blavatsky began to weave a tale of her own mystical life, claiming she spent time in Japan and Tibet (an unlikely claim, as the country was closed to Europeans at the time) and that she had lived through a shipwreck. She also said that her earlier horse-riding accident activated supernatural powers. And she claimed to have met her mysterious "protector," who told her to travel to Tibet to be enlightened. Whether those claims are true or not, Blavatsky finally ended up moving to New York City.

In New York, she met Henry Steel Olcott, a former Civil War soldier and journalist, who was intrigued by Blavatsky and her psychic abilities. By this time, she was dressing how she thought a mystic would, wearing a bright-red tunic and many rings on her fingers and carrying a fur pouch. Olcott was so intrigued, in fact, that he left his wife and family to travel with Blavatsky, who had by now given herself the title "Madame." The pair traveled the country, with Blavatsky performing séances in Spiritualist circles, eventually conducting philosophical salons, where people could discuss ideas about Spiritualism. Eventually, these salons evolved into the Theosophical Society, which would morph into a kind of pseudoreligion led by Madame Blavatsky.

In 1877, Blavatsky wrote *Isis Unveiled* (edited by Olcott), a text she claims was telepathically transmitted to her. The next year, the duo left for India, where they were media darlings—at least for a short time. In Bombay, they published their own journal, the *Theosophist* (which is still in publication today). For a while, Blavatsky and Olcott captivated audiences, probably due in part to their embrace of Eastern religion—and the fact that they vocally denounced colonialism. They held séances publicly and continued writing and publishing their journal. Olcott claimed he was a healer and an expert in magnetism. Their success didn't last long. Emma Coulumb, a woman who had attended a séance, took a job working in Blavatsky's home and then joined the Theosophical Society. Emma apparently became envious of Blavatsky, and the two had a falling-out, which ended with Emma accusing Blavatsky and Olcott of fraudulent séances, going so far as to publish letters accusing them of making it all up.

Eventually, the press turned on them too, calling them frauds, claims bolstered by the Society of Psychical Research, who put out a report to discredit the powers of Madame Blavatsky. Even after her public disgrace, she continued writing, publishing three more books. She died in 1891, during a flu epidemic.

The Theosophical Society is still active today, and people can visit the Blavatsky Lodge in London.

XXXXXX

The Cult of the Occult

In the first half of the twentieth century, Los Angeles was the place where women went to make their dreams come true—and not just dreams of seeing their names in lights. Los Angeles, and to some degree the rest of California, was a mecca for people looking for fresh ways of thinking about the world, especially in the 1920s and '30s. There was the Point Loma Theosophical Society, a community of followers devoted to Madame Blavatsky, located just outside San Diego from 1900 to 1942 (it later moved to Pasadena, where it still operates). There was Krotona, a Theosophy commune in Ojai, founded in the 1920s. Prior to the Ojai community, an earlier version of Krotona lived in a small building in Hollywood that attracted famous names of the day like Charlie Chaplin. This Hollywood occult community was run by Alice Bailey, who frequently spoke on how the world was entering the Age of Aquarius.

Bailey rose to fame through editing the *Messenger*, which was a publication of the Theosophy society out of California. She left the group, though, over disagreements—mainly that she said she was in contact with a Tibetan master who had "ascended," and the others disagreed. Bailey was not deterred; she simply rehashed those old Theosophical ideas and put them into books, beginning with *Initiation: Human and Solar* in 1922. The same year, she began the Lucius

Trust with her husband. She named the trust after Lucifer, whom she associated with bringing knowledge to humanity. In all, Bailey published nineteen books, some of which she claimed were messages channeled from no-longer-living Tibetan religious leaders. Those books stayed in the public imagination for decades. Lou Reed of the Velvet Underground cited the influence of Bailey's 1934 book *A Treatise on White Magic*, calling it "incredible."

It was also in Los Angeles that Aimee Semple McPherson founded her faith-healing evangelical Foursquare Church in the 1920s. McPherson may well have been the first person to run a megachurch in America, with her Angelus Temple, a massive feat of architecture that still sits in Echo Park, where she would preach to audiences numbering close to 10,000.

Then there was the Blackburn cult, sometimes called the Divine Order of the Royal Arms of the Great Eleven, a Los Angeles–based group founded in 1922 by May Otis Blackburn and her daughter Ruth Wieland, who said they had a direct line to speak with angels. They claimed ancient knowledge, including how to resurrect the dead. After setting up a community in Simi Valley, California, the Great Eleven found controversy. First, Ruth's husband mysteriously went missing. Then there were the rumors of strange "healing" rituals, including one in which a paralyzed woman was put into a home-made oven for two days. She did not survive. Unfortunately, hers was not the only death tied to the Great Eleven. The body of Willa Rhoads, a sixteen-year-old girl, was found underneath her parents' floor in their home; she was apparently the victim of a ritual led by Blackburn. Though she was investigated, Blackburn never was imprisoned for either of these deaths. Ultimately, she was found guilty, not of murder or negligence but of defrauding a man out of tens of thousands of dollars. The group collapsed without its leader.

Of course, occult groups weren't only in California. In the first decades of the twentieth century, the nation seemed more open to occult-leaning beliefs. Small pockets of fringe religious groups were born across the country, usually in metropolitan areas. One example is the I AM movement, formed by Edna Ballard, along with her husband, both of whom were converts of Blavatsky's teachings. I AM was a theosophical movement that believed in "Ascended Masters," and adherents sought the masters' divine knowledge as a way to get closer to God. Each group had their own master (Jesus was often considered one), so the teaching varied from group to group. Ballard worked in a small occult bookstore in Chicago and at one point served as editor for *American Occultists*. She was a medium and often claimed she was Joan of Arc reincarnated. Together with her husband, Ballard began the St. Germain Foundation, which still operates today. It's named after St. Germain, an Ascended Master that Guy Ballard claimed to have met in the mountains of California. The Ballards were investigated for mail fraud in 1941.

It's a frequent pattern with these small spiritual groups. They pop up in clusters, often feeding off each other's ideologies (we see it here with so many groups building on Blavatsky's teachings), and with a few notable exceptions they seem to fade out as quickly as they arrive. These groups also highlight a very real potential for fraud and can actively participate in harmful activities, all under the guise of enlightenment and spiritual development. It's important to highlight here that not every group that promotes occult knowledge is bad or harmful—far from it. But we want to be aware of the possibility so that every occult education can be an ethical and loving one.

Evangeline Smith Adams

BRINGING ASTROLOGY TO THE MAINSTREAM

A strology has become such a part of our American culture that its presence is almost a given. Every newspaper and most magazines run some kind of horoscope. Almost everyone knows their sun sign, and a good number of us can rattle off our moon and rising signs too. We even have apps on our phones, like the popular Co–Star, to give us access to all the information the stars can tell us about our lives.

But how did astrology enter our culture so completely?

A lot of the credit goes to Evangeline Smith Adams, who applied entrepreneurial skills to astrology in a bid to raise the practice's profile and support herself. Adams was born in 1868 and grew up in Andover, Massachusetts. She was introduced to astrology through a professor at Boston University. In Boston, she began reading her friends' astrological charts and dabbled in palmistry. Eventually, she turned astrology into a small business, which only grew in scope when she relocated to New York City and found her market.

According to Martin J. Manning in the book *Astrology through History*, Adams was the best-known astrologer in the United States in the early twentieth century. In 1932, *Harper's Monthly* magazine called her the "most comfortably established American astrologer."

What exactly did an established astrologer do? From her tenth floor studio office in Carnegie Hall, Adams had a bustling astrology business of clients who consulted her on everything from money and jobs to romance prospects. Beginning in 1930, WABC hosted her radio show, which ran three times a week at its peak, and reached over one million listeners. The radio show was so popular that Adams got an estimated 4,000 letters a day.

Throughout her career, Adams worked hard to professionalize the field of astrology, treating it as closer to a branch of science than any kind of predatory "fortune-telling." Her client list alone seems to prove her success in bringing astrology into the mainstream, as she advised influential people from celebrities like Mary Pickford and Tallulah Bankhead to the financial experts Charles Schwab and J. P. Morgan. While she may not have advised presidents and First Ladies, as Madame Marcia did, she did claim to be a descendant of John Adams and John Quincy Adams.

She also did a great deal to popularize astrology through skillful marketing. She wrote prolifically, turning out horoscope columns, mail-order readings, and books, including *The Bowl of Heaven*, her 1926 autobiography. In 1927, she started the Astrologers' Guild of America, which aimed to both promote and legally protect practitioners of astrology.

Adams's success did not come easily. At first, she found a lot of resistance. Astrology, though it was by no means new, was not respected at all. In fact, Adams had a hard time setting up her business, because the building proprietors she wanted to rent from wouldn't allow an astrologer to set up shop. For context, over in England, the 1824 Vagrancy Act made astrology a prosecutable crime. Similar laws existed in the States, though most cases were under the more vague umbrella term of *fortune-telling* and not aimed at astrology alone.

Adams ran afoul of local laws against fortune-telling at least twice in her life. In 1914, in New York City, she defended herself in court, making the case that astrology was a science and thus not under the purview of laws against telling fortunes for money. During the trial, she shared an anonymous chart that turned out to have been created for Judge John H. Freschi's son. Manning writes that the judge was impressed by the accuracy of the horoscope and said Adams raised astrology to "the dignity of an exact science." Media accounts of Adams's successful defense in court, as well as her correct prediction of a disaster at the Windsor Hotel, resulted in national fame. As evidence of her growing popularity, in 1928, the *New Yorker* profiled Adams, saying this about her legal issues: "Miss Adams was a public institution. Arresting her was ridiculous." The policewoman who arrested her was given "a light reprimand."

Adams seemed to be able to bridge the divide between the occult world and the business world, a divide traditionally viewed as a schism between women and men. On the one hand, like the Spiritualists, she could make a living pursuing occult activities by providing messages for people seeking answers. On the other hand, she ran her own business outside of her home and was highly sensitive to projecting a professional look in media and marketing photographs. Furthermore, she blended the public's perceptions of science and séance by emphasizing her use of astrological charts for horoscopes, similar to Madame Marcia's decision to shift to astrology to attract higher-paying clients. These women could argue that their messages had a basis in the stars and planets and not another world or the afterlife.

Leonora Piper

The skeptical backlash that eventually brought down the Fox sisters (or, more accurately, inspired Maggie Fox to bring them down herself) targeted many mediums and fortune-tellers, most of them women, toward the end of the nineteenth century. One of the mediums who escaped condemnation as a fraud was Leonora Piper of Boston, Massachusetts. Resigning as head of the American Society for Psychical Research in 1895, the investigator and psychologist William James admitted that Leonora Piper might be a genuine medium, a possible key to understanding communication between the living and the dead. In this speech, James used the analogy of the "white crow" for Piper. He told his audience, "If you wish to upset the law that all crows are black, you mustn't seek to show that no crows are; it is enough if you prove one single crow to be white. . . . My own white crow is Mrs. Piper."

One of the reasons for James's growing acceptance of the *possibility* of Piper's powers was a personal tragedy. James and his family met Piper when in deep mourning over the loss of his young son, Herman, a.k.a. Humster, who died at eighteen months of pneumonia resulting from a whooping cough infection. James and his wife sat with Piper on a recommendation from a family member, and while initially skeptical, James soon changed his mind. In her 2007 book about James, *Ghost Hunters*, journalist Deborah Blum describes

James's creeping suspicions that Piper was legitimate: "It could be that the young psychic knew everyone in his wife's family on sight. She could be incredibly lucky in guessing about the domestic life of strangers and their relatives. Or it could be that most improbable, scientifically impossible conclusion—that this woman 'was possessed of supernormal powers.'" Piper finished the sitting by trying out different names for a recently deceased boy close to the couple, finally settling on Herman.

If people were shocked that William James might be swayed by a medium, they were even more surprised when Richard Hodgson, known as an especially rigorous skeptic, wrote a report in 1897 suggesting that Piper could be the real deal. When Hodgson traveled to Boston in 1888 to help with the reorganization and expansion of the American Society of Psychical Research offices, he set his sights on Piper. He hired private detectives to follow Piper and her family members; they turned up nothing. He checked to see if Piper hired her own investigators to provide information on sitters; she didn't. He surveilled the Piper home to no avail, and he limited the family's newspaper deliveries to days when Piper had no visitors. He observed sittings and prohibited sitters from using their real names.

What pushed Hodgson over the edge into belief was when Piper began communicating with a recently deceased man named George Pellew, who had been a friend of Hodgson's. He came to the conclusion after having 130 sitters, about twenty of whom had known Pellew personally, speak with the spirit. G. P., as the Society called the deceased, identified all but one friend. Though this was enough to sway Hodgson away from skepticism, others weren't so sure. Henry Sidgwick, one of the founders of the British Society for Psychical Research, noted that the spirit could recognize friends, but could not remember much about his life or his "intellectual pursuits."

Blum points out, "Pellew had been an avid student of philosophy; the trance personality barely recognized the subject."

Tellingly, both of these men who had been hardcore skeptics began to believe Piper once they had lost a family member or friend who then was mentioned in or seemed to appear in a sitting. Grief is a powerful emotion that can render someone desperate for contact, whether the deceased was a child or a friend, and mediums know this. Whether or not Leonora Piper was abusing this knowledge of human psychology, she was otherwise a perfect specimen for the investigators. Blum describes Piper as "middle-class respectable." Her husband was a shopkeeper, and the family lived in Beacon Hill. She loved nature and the outdoors. She later told professors G. Stanley Hall and Amy E. Tanner that she lived for the long summer breaks she took from sittings to be in the New England woods. Her Methodist religion had been a comfort to her when she was young, and rather than seeing her trances and spirit communication as a gift, she wanted to know what caused them. She willingly worked with the Psychical Societies, and the majority of her sittings were arranged by handlers for the societies, whether in America or Britain, especially once she became part of the "Cross-Correspondences Study" after Hodgson's death.

This study, which began in late 1906 and continued into 1907, was an intensive effort on the part of the Society for Psychical Research to communicate with members who had passed away, including Edmund Gurney, Richard Hodgson, Henry Sidgwick, and Frederic Myers. Eleanor Sidgwick (who is profiled later in this book) participated as an investigator and researcher. Before the study was organized, an amateur medium and Newnham College lecturer in Cambridge named Margaret Verrall began receiving messages in Greek and Latin from a spirit she believed to be Myers. Around the same time, Piper, in the United States, claimed one of her controls had communicated with Myers. The Society moved Piper to London but kept the two women separated. Piper's ignorance of the classics, both the literature and the languages, made her messages in languages other than English and allusions to poetry more easily believable as spirit communication. Eventually, the study also involved Alice Kipling Fleming, Rudyard Kipling's sister, in India. The three women were kept in their separate locations and psychically passed messages from the society's investigators, past and present, among one another. While there were a few moments when the investigators believed that they experienced connections beyond coincidence, Blum notes that there was plenty of frustration to go around on the parts of the investigators trying to translate the messages and the spirits who were allegedly speaking from the other side.

Piper's sittings for the Psychical Societies, however, weren't the only studies with her willing participation. In the early twentieth century, after Richard Hodgson's spirit had become her new control, she was the subject of a study conducted by psychology professors G. Stanley Hall and Amy E. Tanner. This time, the investigators weren't as accommodating—but we'll hear more about that in the next chapter.

Margaret St. Clair

n the 1960s, Raymond and Rosemary Buckland, initiates of Gardnerian Wicca, brought the new practice to America. This was the beginning of Wicca's spread across the United States, which began its shift from a "rediscovered" fertility cult to a part of the burgeoning feminist political movement. There is evidence, however, that Americans had already been dabbling in Goddess worship as a result of having read Gardner's books and other occult texts, such as the poet Robert Graves's 1948 book *The White Goddess*. In *The White Goddess*, Graves stitched a quilt of various mythologies into a poetic theory of a goddess, or muse, linked to the moon and worshipped by humanity in a distant matriarchal past. One of the Americans most likely reading these texts was the popular pulp magazine science fiction and fantasy writer Margaret St. Clair, and Wicca and the Goddess became integral parts of her writing.

In the updated 1999 edition of Wiccan feminist and environmentalist Starhawk's highly influential 1979 book *The Spiral Dance* (which we discussed in the previous chapter), Starhawk notes her distaste with media representations of witches in a footnote: "We now get trivializing movies like *The Craft* along with the flat-out horror films. Occasionally, a witch shows up on a TV sitcom but is usually portrayed as a wacky, New Age type. I'm waiting for the TV

Witch who happens to be an auto mechanic, an engineer, or a molecular biologist." But this type of everyday witch had already been portrayed in fiction by Margaret St. Clair.

St. Clair was born Eva Margaret Neeley in Kansas in 1911 to a schoolteacher mother and a lawyer father, who later became a US congressman. She was a voracious reader, especially of what would now be considered science fiction. In 1919, her father passed away, leaving her and her mother to move first to Lawrence, Kansas, and then, in 1928, to California, where she completed undergraduate and master's degrees at the University of California at Berkeley. While at university, she married children's book author Eric St. Clair.

In the 1940s and 1950s, Margaret St. Clair was a prolific writer of genre stories for pulp magazines. It was while she was doing research in the 1950s that she most likely encountered Gerald Gardner's 1949 novel *High Magic's Aid* and his 1954 book *Witchcraft Today*—a decade before the Bucklands brought Gardnerian Wicca to America. St. Clair and her husband were intrigued by the neo-paganism movement, in particular Wicca. For a while, they were seekers and do-it-yourselfers, corresponding with the Bucklands and reading widely. Margaret and Eric were later initiated by the Bucklands in 1966, using the Craft names Froniga and Weyland.

While there are hints of neo-paganism and Wicca throughout Margaret St. Clair's fiction, her use of Wiccan symbols and themes intensified in her later work, such as her 1963 book *Sign of the Labrys*. (This novel was also part of the inspiration behind Dungeons and Dragons, the role-playing game that became embroiled in the Satanic Panic but survived to remain popular today.) St. Clair didn't just use Wiccan ideas wholesale, though; sometimes she interpreted them in a way that she may have found more appealing. Pagan historian Chas Clifton reports that Buckland, while he liked *Labrys*, did

"Occasionally, a witch shows up on a TV sitcom but is usually portrayed as a wacky, New Age type. I'm waiting for the TV Witch who happens to be an auto mechanic, an engineer, or a molecular biologist."

—Starhawk, *The Spiral Dance*

give St. Clair "a mild slap on the wrist for 'giving away too much'" and disapproved of her having a man initiate another man in the novel. Gardner's theology was glaringly heteronormative. He was insistent in *Witchcraft Today* that only partners of the opposite sex could initiate and work with each other in the circle, because that was what his fellow coven members told him was necessary for polarity and the creation of energy. According to Gardner and his informants, this work usually would result in intimate relationships between partners, and they identified initiation partnerships between men to be an error committed by other occult groups, such as the Knights Templar. Today, that view has changed—but Margaret St. Clair could already imagine possibilities beyond it, even in the 1960s.

In *Sign of the Labrys*, St. Clair created a post-apocalyptic world in which people are still reeling from a pandemic caused by the proliferation of various yeasts. People such as the main character, Sam Sewell, live in underground bunkers, avoiding one another for fear of catching or spreading illness. When a government agent demands that Sam give up his friend Despoina, the head of a resistance group whose members claim they can use magic, Sam is confused because he has never met this woman. He reluctantly leaves his routine and goes in search of Despoina and her group through the mazelike subterranean levels. Along the way, he learns more about what happened to society and what remains of it.

St. Clair describes Despoina and her comrades as Wiccans, including rituals like a Sabbat; Gardnerian nudity and scourging; the use of the ceremonial athame dagger and the ritual circle; a man in a mask with horns, most likely representing the Horned God; and the use of altered states of mind and spellcraft, to name just a few aspects. Furthermore, as the coven comes together, Sam becomes the High Priest, or the Devil, to Despoina's High Priestess, and, like

Gardner's idea of the Great Rite, they consummate their relationship. Murray and Gardner had reported that Christians interpreted the High Priest role as the Devil, a likely source for St. Clair's use of the term.

So, what of Starhawk's wish to see more everyday witches represented? In St. Clair's fiction, her witches usually have day jobs, and they live in her fictional worlds without much, if any, surprise on the part of the other characters. In *Labrys*, for instance, Sam meets a scientist in the lower levels who helps him on his quest. That scientist worked in a laboratory in the "Before Times," but she also is part of Despoina's coven. She flows seamlessly from scientific experimentation to the Craft and back, thereby illustrating how Wicca can become the spiritual part of a practicing witch's otherwise ordinary life. These characters also work individually and together with their coven to protest the government system in power, both before the pandemic, when they saw that atomic annihilation was possible, and post-pandemic, when humankind has fractured even more into despair and the rise of a police state is imminent.

And that is probably one of the most striking things about St. Clair's fiction. While she weaves her interest in pagan religion throughout her works to varying degrees depending upon the story she is telling, those interests become a part of the surrounding story and part of her characters' accepted, everyday lives. There is nothing shocking in St. Clair's work when a woman identifies as a witch. For St. Clair's characters, mundane domesticity can coexist with fantastic creatures, complex AI, warring corporate factions, and magic. This multigenre grab bag of stories may not be easily classifiable, but it may have been St. Clair's attempt to portray the complexity of our world as it was and as it could be.

Lorraine Warren

THE DEVIL MADE THEM DO IT

The occult hasn't entered into a court of law since the Salem witch trials—with a few notable exceptions. In 1974, Michael Taylor of Ossett in Yorkshire, England, made headlines when he was found not guilty of murdering his wife, Catherine. The details of the crime are gruesome. Taylor was seen after the murder running naked down the street of his neighborhood, covered in his wife's blood. He had torn out her eyes and tongue. There was little doubt that he killed his wife, so why was he found not guilty? A jury in Leeds found Taylor to be insane. But it wasn't the violent nature of the crime that made the headlines—it was what came before the murder. Taylor had been deemed possessed and had undergone an exorcism, one that lasted a long seven hours. Newspapers reported that Taylor had forty demons living within his body at one time. Ultimately, it was insanity that made his defense, not exorcism, but in the court of public opinion, the Devil made him do it.

The Devil did become a legitimate defense strategy in 1981, when the trial of Arne Johnson became the first court case to use a "Devil made me do it" defense. At the heart of this case are Ed and Lorraine Warren, a married couple famous for being demonologists (and in Lorraine's case, a medium). They claimed to be investigators, but critics have contended that they were biased at best, especially since they seemed to sensationalize their investigations. For a long time, they ran a museum out of their Connecticut home, the Warrens' Occult Museum, which displayed haunted and possessed objects they had collected over the years, including the infamous Annabelle, a Raggedy Ann doll, which the Warrens displayed behind thick glass (they reasoned that the demon-possessed doll was too dangerous to be touched by humans). As a clairvoyant, Lorraine also appeared on several television shows, including *Paranormal State* and *The Scariest Places on Earth*. She served as a consultant on the film *The Conjuring*, which was based on their investigations, and she was given a cameo in the movie. The Conjuring movies spawned so many titles that the Warrens practically have a shared movie universe. Whether oversensationalized or not, the couple did look into many reportedly haunted places and numerous possession cases. Together, they investigated notable cases of the paranormal, like the *Amityville Horror* house, the haunting of the Annabelle doll (which, like Amityville, spawned numerous movies), and the Enfield poltergeist.

But it was the Arne Johnson case that brought the Warrens into the court of law.

Johnson was accused of stabbing his landlord, Alan Bono. In court, Johnson's lawyers said they had "proof" that Johnson had contracted demons in an earlier exorcism. According to reports, Johnson's girlfriend's young brother, David Glatzel, was possessed by a demon. The Catholic Church performed a church-sanctioned exorcism, with Johnson present, which was when the demon left the child's body and entered Johnson. The demon then turned Johnson violent, resulting in Bono's death. Ultimately, though the case made history for its unique defense, the strategy didn't work, and Johnson was convicted of manslaughter.

The Warrens investigated the Glatzel case and came to Johnson's defense following the murder, upholding all of the possession claims. They spoke directly to the police shortly after the crime to explain that Johnson was indeed under the influence of a demon. The Glatzel family, however, was less than welcoming of the Warrens following the high-profile case, especially as the Warrens seemed to profit from the tragedy, publishing a book about the proceedings by Gerald Brittle (the case was also adapted to film, once in 1983 in a made-for-television movie and again in 2021 with the third installment in the Conjuring series, titled *The Conjuring: The Devil Made Me Do It*). In 2006, David Glatzel's brother, Carl, sued Brittle and Lorraine Warren when Brittle's book was going into a reprint. Carl Glatzel claimed that the Warrens, using Brittle, took advantage of his family for monetary gain. In 2007, Glatzel told the Associated Press that "It was living hell when we were kids [. . .] It was just a nightmare. I'm not going to go through that again. Neither is my brother." He also said that "his brother had suffered from mental illness as a child but has now recovered." The lawsuit was dropped, but the book reprint was stopped due to the legal issues. Still, as evidenced by the 2021 film, this case is still irrevocably tied to the Warrens and to the supernatural. Occult narratives are difficult to shake in the public's mind, and those narratives can have real and devastating effects, particularly for women.

"She's Not Alive, Honey"

Sylvia Browne was a psychic who rose to fame through her appearances on radio and television, including weekly stints on *The Montel Williams Show* for a while. Browne, an older woman with a deep, scratchy voice, was less of a performer than some other high-profile psychics. Instead of animatedly speaking to a crowd or enthusiastically delivering news of loved ones visiting us from beyond, Browne was known for her monotone, sometimes one- or two-word answers. She didn't always want to assure people that their loved ones had "crossed over" and were happy in their afterlife.

This was part of her plan, as she explained in an interview with the *Guardian*: "I don't think people should go to a psychic to hear a fairy story. . . . It might be nice for a time, but what about the validity in the future." The only problem? Browne's results weren't valid at all.

Take the Shawn Hornbeck case. In 2002, Sylvia Browne was asked about the eleven-year-old boy who had gone missing while out riding his bike. Browne said he had died, and more, he was buried between two boulders. The only problem? Hornbeck was alive and still in the clutches of his kidnapper. In this case, the FBI was able to follow the investigation to the home of Mike Devlin, where Hornbeck was rescued along with another kidnapped boy.

Had the parents and law enforcement taken Browne at her word, the search for a kidnapped boy could have turned to a search for a grave in a wooded area. And Hornbeck's future could've been very different.

This is basically what happened to Amanda Berry in 2004. Louwana Miller went on *The Montel Williams Show* to ask Sylvia Browne about her missing daughter. Browne said flatly, "She's not alive, honey." Miller gave up hope, according to the press, and eventually died thinking her daughter was dead. But in May 2013, Amanda Berry was found alive at the Cleveland home of Ariel Castro, where she and two other women had been imprisoned for up to eleven years. Would this living nightmare have ended sooner if Browne hadn't encouraged Berry's mother, and the public, to stop searching? We can't know for sure, but it's clear that celebrity psychics' "connections" to the other side can have real-world and dangerous consequences.

Sylvia Browne did get indicted for fraud once—but not for misleading the parents of Shawn Hornbeck and Amanda Berry, or the viewers of *Montel Williams*. It was for selling securities in a gold-mining operation and funneling the money into the Nirvana Foundation for Psychical Research, which she ran with her husband at the time.

Miss Cleo

THE PSYCHIC FRIEND IN YOUR TV

Anyone who owned a television in the late 1990s knows her name. Miss Cleo was a staple of television advertising, a friendly face to keep insomniacs company on late nights or to greet latchkey kids in the afternoons once school let out. She was a welcoming presence, even in her short commercials for the Psychic Readers Network, with her big smile and gentle Jamaican patois. On those commercials, as she consulted her tarot cards, callers would ask questions like, "Who is the father of my baby?" It was a thirty-second Maury Povich talk show. She promised that she could answer your questions, which she did with her loud, no-nonsense way of talking. For instance, once, when a woman called in about improving her love life, Miss Cleo flipped over the cards and flatly told her caller to stop the 2 a.m. booty calls. She was

a mix of your cool best friend, your worldly aunt who would tell you anything you wanted to know, and an all-knowing oracle. In short, Miss Cleo was an instant celebrity. And she could be your best friend—for a few minutes, at a few dollars each minute.

Miss Cleo was born Youree Dell Harris, not in Jamaica but in Los Angeles, where she was raised—though she always claimed she had Jamaican roots. Growing up, she attended an all-girls Catholic school, a community she never quite felt fully accepted in, largely because she was a lesbian. In a 2006 interview with the *Advocate*, she called her sexuality "the pink elephant in the room." Her family and close friends knew that she was a lesbian, but she wasn't fully out. Society, she said, wasn't ready for her: "I never felt bad, but I knew society didn't accept me. This was the '70s. Things were changing, but they weren't all that changed." She married a man at age nineteen, only to be divorced by twenty-one. Following that, she lived as a lesbian, though she still didn't come out publicly. Mainstream society may not have been ready to accept her LGBTQ lifestyle, but her family was.

In a 2014 interview with *Vice*, Miss Cleo described the tradition she grew up in: Obeah, a religion similar to Haitian Vodou that developed in the West Indies, introduced by enslaved people from Africa in the seventeenth century. She says she was trained by a Haitian mambo, a female Obeah priest, to be a mambo herself. It took her three decades to achieve the title. As a mambo, she would act as a bridge between the spiritual world and the physical one, but she was never a "psychic"—that phrase was only given to her by the handlers of the Psychic Readers Network, who told her that anything related to voodoo would scare audiences. Still, she always maintained that her occult practices and interactions with the spirit world were very real.

For Miss Cleo, the occult community was a village, a safe place. It was a community that she not only belonged in, but felt responsible for. She took her role as spiritual advisor seriously. In various interviews, she described the occult community as a found family for her; she took care of them and they took care of her.

The occult was also lucrative for Miss Cleo—at first. There were the infomercials, of course, for the phone psychic business. Soon, there was a web-based psychic business. And her own line of products: tarot cards for the at-home mediums, apparel, and a 2001 book titled *Keepin' It Real: A Practical Guide for Spiritual Living*, her smile beaming on the front cover.

Her success didn't last long.

In February 2002, the Federal Trade Commission targeted the Psychic Readers Network—and Miss Cleo, specifically—for deceptive business practices and false advertising. They alleged the network took over $1 billion from customers by offering "free" readings to phone clients only to hit them with astronomical bills.

Miss Cleo, for her part, was only a spokesperson. The FTC eventually dropped her name from any investigations, and the owners of the company, Steven Feder and Peter Stolz, settled out of court for $500 million. But the damage to Miss Cleo's reputation was already done. The court of public opinion labeled her a fraud, and she quietly slipped from the public eye. She did, however, continue her spiritual consultation business with private customers, which generated enough income for her to comfortably raise two daughters.

She appeared in the documentary film *Hotline* in 2014, in which she detailed her involvement with the phone psychic business. In it, she described how the predatory business ruined her reputation, but also how most of the psychics working the phone lines got cents on the dollar. They weren't the ones getting rich; they were only trying to make ends meet. "Those people are not the bad guys," she said in the documentary, "even if they weren't great psychics."

In 2016, Miss Cleo passed away from cancer at the age of fifty-three.

Stormy Daniels

You may remember Stormy Daniels as the adult film star who made headlines after she received money in 2016 from Donald Trump's lawyer, allegedly at Trump's behest, in order to keep her quiet about an affair. (She kept quiet only until 2018, when news of the affair, the nondisclosure agreement, and the possibly illegal payment hit the press; she then said things about his genitals we won't repeat.) Daniels has now begun a new supernatural adventure, following what she called "unexplainable experiences" that she has had throughout her life. In 2020, she founded Spooky Babes, a team that investigates (and as their website says, sometimes debunks) paranormal activity. The team, which is made up of Daniels, various mediums, psychics, and skeptics, and a haunted doll named Susan, travels to haunted locations and attempts to make contact.

Spooky Babes, which isn't currently affiliated with a TV channel or streaming service, is part of a tradition of ghost-hunting shows, most of which are overwhelmingly male. The first of these shows to really spark public interest was *Ghost Hunters*, which premiered in 2004. The team was from TAPS, The Atlantic Paranormal Society, and was led by two men, Jason Hawes and Grant Wilson. Hawes and Wilson were unlikely celebrities. They were Roto-Rooter plumbers by day, but at night they became occult scientists, armed with recording devices and EMF meters and ready to find ghosts wherever they might hide. Audiences particularly responded to their desire to debunk. These ghost hunters always tried to find a "real world" reason for the haunting. After all, most likely a ghost was really just a drafty window or a door that was hung crooked.

The success of *Ghost Hunters* ushered in a deluge of other ghost hunting shows: *Paranormal State*, *Most Haunted*, *Ghost Hunters: International*, just to name a few. But more interesting (for our purposes) than the sheer volume of ghost-finding shows are the people who are finding those ghosts. The overwhelming majority of people on camera in these paranormal-investigation-style shows are men; more specifically, they are white men. Rather than focus on the emotional aspect of the psychic business, these ventures existed to take a scientific (or to better describe them, a pseudoscientific) look at the phenomenon of ghosts—and culturally, we tend to associate science and rationality with masculinity.

We see this reflected in how these shows talk about communicating with ghosts. There seems to be a kind of performative machismo with words like *hunting* for communicating with spirits. There's also a focus on factual evidence (or at least the pursuit of those facts, however performative that search might be). And with this focus on science, we can truly see the gender divide in these occult reality shows. Most of these shows do now feature some women on the team, but the lineups remain mostly male.

This is where women like Daniels are important, especially for gender parity in the supernatural space. In the trailer for *Spooky Babes* (available on YouTube), Daniels is seen with her team, composed of women and men. As the Spooky Babes investigate, Daniels herself acts as a kind of medium or conduit for the spirits. In her own words, "I see dead people."

Female mediums are by no means new, but as we've seen before, mediumship is a useful way for women who are disenfranchised from society to leverage power. This seems an increasingly apt way to consider Daniels. We can't not discuss the fact that Daniels is a former porn star and stripper, one who rose to infamy when she reportedly slept with a married Donald Trump (while his wife was pregnant) and took money from him in order to keep their affair secret. Our culture has never been kind to women who chose to work in the sex industry, and Daniels was no exception. After the scandal broke, Trump was elected president, while she was ridiculed and degraded in the public arena.

When viewed in this context, Daniels's new career in the paranormal seems to be a way for her to control the narrative of her own story. Daniels says that she got into supernatural investigations following a series of paranormal encounters in her New Orleans home. She says those experiences "led me to want to prove that the things I was experiencing and feeling and seeing were real." In other words, she needed to both validate her own experiences and form a connection with those around her. The show seems to want audiences to empathize with Daniels, which puts one clip of the show in an interesting light, when a blindfolded Daniels hears a ghost yell "slut" at her. The clip, from an online teaser for *Spooky Babes*, cuts away before Daniels can answer, but we can only hope that she told that ghost exactly what she thought of that word.

Daniels isn't the only woman using occult investigation as a way to seize hold of her image and establish herself as canny, sensitive, and more than a pretty face. Bridget Marquardt and Holly Madison, former girlfriends of *Playboy*'s Hugh Hefner and stars of the reality show *The Girls Next Door*, made news in 2019 when they apparently contacted the spirit of Hefner (who died in 2017) during a séance led

Women have never had easy access to power, whether political, religious, or economic. In the court of public opinion, women face harsher judgments when they make choices or behave in ways that don't follow cultural expectations. The occult, then, becomes one pathway for women to grab power and control the narrative. Women have used this fringe spiritual space to step into areas previously off-limits to them. And sometimes, when they made these moves, they discovered they could become famous, or at least infamous.

In the 1920s and 1930s, Evangeline Adams, for example, turned her interest in astrology into a nationwide business, and her clientele gave her reach into the wealthiest homes in America. Or, in a different and more contemporary scenario, we can look at someone like Stormy Daniels. Through her internet show, Daniels used the occult to change her personal brand. It's a powerful move.

There are many women who have realized that an embrace of the occult persona is one of the most powerful statements one can make. It's a kind of rebellion, daring society to come at you with all they have. But, as we will see in the next chapter, there will always be those who are opposed to the occult for one reason or another.

4

PARANORMAL INVESTIGATION

CHALLENGING THE OCCULT

f some women are seizing power by embracing the occult, it stands to reason there will always be others who want to separate themselves from the pack by rejecting it, or by using the occult as an accusation. Some women take power by taking on the identity of the skeptic, both to understand the occult more fully but also to educate the public on its possible harms.

We know that a lot of the mediums of the Spiritualist period were making it up. The performances were just that—performances for an audience. Journalist Mary Roach, in her 2006 book investigating the afterlife, *Spook*, details how the mediums of the late nineteenth and early twentieth centuries used cheesecloth (and sometimes animal organs) to trick their customers into thinking they were seeing the ectoplasm of the ghosts in the room. There was also some speculation that these mediums were using the hands of corpses taken from local hospitals as the touch of hands from beyond. Critics worried that these psychics were preying on vulnerable people. Imagine the worst moment of your life: you've lost a child or someone else close to you. You are lost in despair . . . until someone says that they can reunite you for a moment. You can hear from, or maybe even see, your lost son or daughter. For a price.

On the one hand, if it lessens the grief and helps with the process, what is the harm? The séance is akin to therapy, then, and may be worth the time and the money. But in the worst of cases, it is predatory. It is someone callously defrauding the most vulnerable of people.

The history of occult acceptance is not a straightforward timeline. For every step forward, there have been more than a few steps back. In our research journey, we found it important to look at those women who were pushing back against the occult and, more importantly, to examine their reasons for doing so.

In this chapter, you will learn a bit of the history of the debunkers, the ghost hunters, and the societies that formed to investigate claims of the paranormal, as well as why they were taking on this kind of work. For some, it was about the pursuit of science, trying to find a rational explanation for the supernatural. For others, it was an ethical imperative. Their main mission was to root out fraud and keep criminals from conning people out of money.

Illusionist Harry Houdini, who is a background character here (though he pops up a lot!), understood intimately how fake mediums can prey on grief. He began his campaign to investigate supernatural practitioners because he was hopeful that he could speak to his late father. When that proved impossible, he made a career of uncovering the tricks that these fraudulent mediums and psychics would use.

Later in his life, Houdini worried about mediums misrepresenting him after death. He feared that psychics would say they "channeled" his spirit and they would say things using his voice, things he never would say in life. Again, this seems potentially harmless; it can be comforting if a psychic says that your grandmother is coming through and she is proud of you. Those words can be treasured. Ventriloquizing the dead can even be beneficial to society—if, say, a medium claims to channel a famous figure like Benjamin Franklin, and he says he wants the nation to free enslaved people or give women votes. Isn't this harmless, or even positive? These channeled voices can give legitimacy to a speaker who doesn't have it in the eyes of society. But unfortunately, this can be a double-edged sword. What if a medium appropriates someone's voice and uses it to communicate a message that the person would never have supported? This kind of ventriloquism is a violation of human identity at the very basic level. People should not lose control over their own image, life's story, or voice following their death.

This hints at the real fear that Houdini spoke about prior to his death. He was worried—for good reason—that fake mediums would misrepresent him and his ideas following his death. To protect himself, he told his wife, Bess, that if communication after death was really possible, he would contact her using a prearranged code. Bess held annual séances for ten years after his death and never made a verifiable contact (one "spirit" did give her the right code, but it was shown to be a fraud). To this day, stage magicians try to contact Houdini every year, without success.

In this book, we have shown how women have used the occult to engage in political and cultural rebellion, gaining power where they previously had none. But saying that women used the occult to achieve influence or independence is not the same as saying they always *embraced* the occult, or held it in a positive light. Some worked with skeptics like Houdini—or even with Houdini himself—to investigate and debunk psychic phenomena. Others allied themselves with more sinister anti-occultism movements. In 1690s Salem, for example, the young girls who accused the witches were steeped in their society's religious beliefs. Whether or not they believed their own words, those stories were able to flourish because their community's worldview was starkly black-and-white. There was good, which meant that evil also had to exist. We see something similar in the Satanic Panic, nearly three hundred years later. One woman's terrifying story of abuse grew into a fear of the Devil that pervaded schools, homes, and neighborhoods. At times, even when we desire to protect the most vulnerable among us, hysteria and irrationality can take hold and breed chaos, to the point of harming the innocent. These groups were so terrified of a perceived evil that they would sacrifice everything to keep themselves and their loved ones safe.

But as we will see with some of these movements, that instinct to protect went too far. By contrast, investigators and skeptics did indeed uncover real fraud, which did protect vulnerable people. The detractors in this section, as you will see, swing from imaginary witch hunts to real scientific investigation.

In this chapter, we will introduce you to some of the women who have taken a stand, rightly or wrongly, against occult activity. Sometimes, this comes in the form of accusations against innocent people. At other times, it comes in the form of calling out the fake psychics, mediums, and other magicians who exploit people's pain and take their money. Seeing the powerful potential of the occult doesn't always mean that we accept every part of it. Skeptics play an important part in keeping the occult world ethical.

Ann Putnam Jr. & Abigail Williams

THE ACCUSERS OF SALEM

n January 1692, the Devil came to Salem.

Betty Parris, the nine-year-old daughter of Reverend Samuel Parris, was the first child to fall mysteriously ill. Her cousin, Abigail Williams, who lived with the Parrises, soon succumbed to the same sickness. The girls ran fevers and had seizures, their bodies contorting with pain. They seemed terrified of something unseen. They sometimes hid under pieces of furniture, as if they could conceal themselves from their unknown assailant.

Soon, the affliction spread to other young girls in the area: Mary Walcott, Ann Putnam Jr., Elizabeth Hubbard, Elizabeth Booth, Mercy Lewis, Susannah Sheldon, Mary Warren. They all complained of terrible pains shooting through their fever-ravaged bodies. They claimed that some unseen force—a specter of a person—was torturing them day and night. Family members watched in horror as the girls were pinched and bitten by something invisible. Their bodies arched in unnatural ways. Their necks bent at terrible angles. Their backs contorted into shapes that shouldn't be humanly possible. Finally, the families could bear no more of the girls' anguished screams.

Worried, the reverend called in a doctor, who was unable to find anything physically wrong with the girls. The problem, then, must be supernatural. They were bewitched.

When questioned about who was torturing them, the girls were reluctant to speak up. Then, Ann Putnam Jr. and Abigail Williams began talking, specifically naming two women: Sarah Good and Sarah Osborne.

Once they began telling their story, it grew from there. The girls, at least according to the stories they told, were lured into the dangerous realm of satanic magic by Tituba, an enslaved woman working for the Parrises, who taught the girls how to do magic rituals to divine details about their future husbands. It was harmless fun . . . at first. But Betty soon claimed that she began to dream of a dark shadowy man—the Devil—coming to her in her sleep. He asked her to join forces with him and sign her soul away.

By the end of February, three women were accused of witchcraft: Sarah Good, Sarah Osborne, and Tituba. On March 1, they were arrested and examined, with Ann Putnam Jr.'s father, Thomas Putnam, acting as court clerk. Tituba confirmed the girls' story. Four more women were added to the accused list that month. In April, the list grew even longer.

By the summer, the witchcraft accusations burned through Salem village and into the neighboring towns. All in all, more than 200 women, men, and children were accused.

The witchcraft hysteria caught on for many reasons: spiritual, cultural, political, even interpersonal. The religious fervor of influential Puritan minister and writer Cotton Mather was perhaps the most obvious factor. Like his contemporaries, Mather associated the Devil with the New World and its Indigenous population. In his books and sermons he portrayed the colonists as targets of the Devil because they brought Christianity to the wilderness (as he would describe it). And the Devil didn't just have demons—he had witches as his foot soldiers. These witches, who could be anyone in town, sold their souls and signed the Devil's book—New Englanders were obsessed with the idea of sealed satanic covenants in books. Witches could commit many blasphemous acts, though they seemed to lean toward seduction and property damage. Moreover, if pious neighbors, usually young women, refused to be recruited to the dark side and sign that book, they quickly regretted their refusal. They would be afflicted with fits, convulsions, the irresistible desire to mock religion and men in charge using foul language, and other tortures like bites and pins stuck into their skin. Some afflicted girls were said to vomit pins and nails. These sights all over town, and in the meeting house during trials, terrified people into paranoia. Ironically, Mather even admitted that the Devil could use fears of witches to drive people to destroy their own community: "But in the meantime, the Devil improves the Darkness of this Affair, to push us into a Blind Mans Buffet, and we are even ready to be sinfully, yea, hotly, and madly, mauling one another in the dark."

All of this confusion and terror made sense to Mather because, in addition to his belief that Satan was looking to snare innocents and that witchcraft was real, he believed he was living in the "End Times." In the 1680s in Massachusetts, there was a political crisis. The colonists had rebelled against a royal governor, and, in retaliation, England's Lords of Trade voided their charter. There were several years of social and legal uncertainty as political tides shifted in England and in the colonies. Mather and his father, Increase, publicly worked to transition the people through this period, and Increase became involved in negotiating for the new charter. In addition to the political chaos, the community was suffering smallpox epidemics and other local disasters including home-destroying fires, all leading to the general feeling of impending doom. Observing the upheaval around him, Cotton Mather did some back-of-the-envelope math and figured out that Christ was coming back in 1697. His calculations were off (not just because the world is still going today, but because the actual math was wrong), but he and others of the time truly did believe that the end was nigh, and furthermore that the world's final years would be an intensely dangerous moment of demonic depredation. It would be the Devil's last chance to do some diabolical damage, just as the apocalypse was described in the Bible.

In addition to the political and social turmoil, there was an ever-present fear of attack by Native Americans. Many colonial families in the Salem area had experienced losses in King Philip's War of 1675 to 1678 with the Wampanoag people. Some inhabitants of Salem village were refugees from the Maine frontier where there were numerous skirmishes. These attacks were primarily motivated by the settlers invading and taking over Indigenous lands and violating agreements they'd made with local Native groups. Today we understand these battles as a response to colonialist violence, but the Puritans believed that God mandated their property expansion and that the Indigenous people were in league with the Devil. The colonists also feared attacks from the French, with whom they were in competition for land and resources.

Beneath all of these traumas, fears, confusions, and intense spiritual manias, there was another insidious factor helping to fuel the flames of persecution: internal dissension. Salem village was rife with quarrels and grudges that surfaced in the "evidence" in the trials. The hiring process for new ministers often led to heated factions within the village that the larger town of Salem would have to mediate, and the turnover rate of ministers was high. These men of God would complain of lack of pay and lack of firewood. One of the executed witches, described as the ringleader of the coven, was former minister George Burroughs, who had, years previously, left the village for Maine shrouded in a cloud of acrimony.

There were also land-boundary disputes and quarrels over loose animals damaging property. One example of this is the case of Rebecca Nurse. She was in her seventies and quite ill when she was accused, not exactly in good shape for cavorting with Satan—but in fact, the accusations most likely stemmed from a property dispute that didn't initially have anything to do with her. Her loudest accusers were members of the Putnam family, who swore ten out of eighteen depositions against her—a degree of targeting that might seem hard to explain, if you didn't know that the Putnams and the Nurses had a long-standing family quarrel. Rebecca's parents had settled in the neighboring town of Topsfield, and there were several legal battles over the border of their property with the Putnams' in Salem village. Ill will was still simmering in 1692. Despite her reputation for kindness, her age and illness, her partial deafness, and a cadre of vocal supporters, Nurse was found guilty—*after* an initial finding of not guilty, which Judge William Stoughton pressured the jury to reconsider. She was taken to her congregation in chains to be publicly excommunicated before her execution. Like their British and continental forebears, the Puritans made the investigations, trials, excommunications, and executions into community spectacles.

In America, as in England and Europe during earlier witch-hunting crazes, women who were widows, unmarried, poor or possibly itinerant, or existing on the margins of town would be early targets. These individuals, usually older women, could be seen as a burden during hard agricultural seasons, or after wars, like King Philip's War. If they didn't get along with fellow citizens, they had no support against accusation. We see this with the first three women accused in Salem: Sarah Good, Sarah Osborne, and Tituba. Tituba was an enslaved woman brought from the West Indies by Reverend Parris. Good was not well-liked in Salem. In her teens, her father committed suicide, and his estate didn't fall to her. Later, she lost a husband and gained debts. When she was accused, the villagers viewed her as a beggar. She didn't have a stable address, and she didn't always live with her second husband. The villagers were suspicious of her because they thought she was insulting and quarrelsome and that she cursed farm animals. A court reporter wrote that Good's answers during questioning were delivered "in a very spiteful and wicked manner," which doesn't seem to be very objective reporting.

Good supported the accusations against Osborne, maybe to deflect attention to someone else. Osborne also was the target of rumors of illicit and rude behavior. After the death of her husband, she engaged in protracted legal battles with the Putnams over her inheritance, not unlike Rebecca Nurse. Neither Good nor Osborne were regular church attendees. Tituba, who had never had contact with the Puritan legal system up until that moment, was, by all accounts, a faithful Christian. She was accused by twelve-year-old Ann Putnam Jr. and not the girls in Parris's household with whom she seemed to have had a good relationship. She made a lengthy confession, most likely out of sheer terror at finding herself in this dangerous situation and an acute awareness of her lack of power and social position.

These three women, and the individuals to follow, all were damned, to some extent, by bitter and venomous hostilities that had been brewing in Salem for years. Finding out the town had a witch coven made up of hundreds of members was just the match to a flammable pile of animosities, fears, and insults. There were no actual witches anywhere near Salem, but the story, supported by the religious and legal system, gave cover for murder. One of the judges for the trials, John Hathorne, even said explicitly during an interrogation that he was influenced by the insider status of the accusers relative to the marginalized accused. He couldn't believe the accused could be innocent because that would make the accusers, who had young girls in their ranks, murderers.

Bridget Bishop was the first one brought to trial. Despite her pleas of innocence, Bishop was also the first one executed, sentenced to hanging. She died on June 10, 1692, near Salem's Gallows Hill.

When the trials ended, nineteen people had been hanged (fourteen women and five men). One man had been pressed to death by stones. Two dogs were killed as well. The details surrounding the dogs are hazy at best, but animals could be bewitched or be a witch's familiar. Either way, they were yet more innocent victims of the chaos.

As the trials continued, the accused rose in economic position and public stature, disturbing the powers that be. More middle- to upper-class couples who ran businesses, like the Proctors and the Englishes, were named. The Englishes left town. The Proctors were given death sentences. John Proctor was hanged. Elizabeth Proctor was reprieved by her pregnancy. At the end, several ministers were accused, especially ones who called the trials into question, and the governor's wife was accused.

For many reasons, including the general feeling that things ran out of control, many people began to question the whole process. People involved with the trials, like the men on the jury and one of the judges, Samuel Sewall, began to express a guilty uncertainty about verdicts. The mania melted away into anger and shame. Things didn't return to normal, though. They couldn't. The accusers and the accused were living in the same village. The accused who had been jailed and survived now owed payment for the time spent in jail. Most of the accused had lost all of their possessions and property to overzealous and corrupt officials. Survivors were weighed down with loss and physical and emotional trauma. Many survivors and their families and the families of the executed, like the Nurses, worked for years to receive pardons or apologies.

Illustrating just how difficult this process could be is the case of Elizabeth Johnson Jr. of Andover, Massachusetts. Accused in 1692 and sentenced to death in 1693, Johnson was granted a reprieve when the governor ended the debacle. Although she didn't face her death sentence, she still hadn't received a pardon in 2021 when she became the focus of an eighth-grade class's civics project. The students, according to their teacher Carrie LaPierre, were learning about acceptance of people who may be different from themselves. They were moved by Johnson's plight and made seeking her pardon part of their class project.

Ministers and government officials wrangled for another ten years after the Salem trials over the validity of spectral evidence. This type of evidence had been used in the trials to show that the witches could send their spirits, or images, to torment accusers while the witch appeared to be sitting idly or even sleeping. The Puritans didn't completely give up on believing that people's ghosts could be seen flitting around doing bad things. They just decided, over the course of the trials and into the eighteenth century, that the Devil was sneaky and nasty enough to produce images of innocent Christians doing evil when they actually weren't, which really undermined the evidence for the executions.

In 1706, a twenty-seven-year-old Ann Putnam Jr. made a confession before the Salem church so she could join. Ann had been one of the more tenacious and prolific of the accusers when she was twelve, having claimed to have been afflicted by sixty-two people, and she testified under oath against seventeen of the nineteen executed persons. Additionally, she was a member of the Putnam family, making it likely that she and her mother, Ann Putnam Sr., who also claimed to have been afflicted, were mouthpieces for Putnam grudges. As a twelve-year-old girl, Ann would have been powerless enough to be manipulated or precocious enough to rebel against her tightly structured life, or maybe a bit of both.

Her confession was approved by Rebecca Nurse's son. She asked for forgiveness, describing what happened as a "delusion," though she didn't seem to fully take responsibility for her actions; she reminded the congregation many times that she was not the only accuser, and ultimately blamed her delusions on "the powers of darkness," just as she had originally blamed her affliction on women in league with Satan. Her apology seemed to emphasize that she was an "instrument" of something else. She didn't quite admit to deliberately lying or conspiring with the other girls to accuse the innocent, but she didn't exactly not say that, either.

The Witch-Hunter's Bible

I t's hard to know with precision how many people were accused and executed as witches in the sixteenth and seventeenth centuries in Europe. Most recent estimations put the number around 100,000 accusations and 50,000 executions, with some putting the executed as high as 100,000 and the accusations at 200,000. And more than 80 percent of them were women.

Why did women face a greater risk of being accused, prosecuted, and executed? To answer this question, we must look at the *Malleus Maleficarum* (first published in 1486), a key text that witch-hunters used to find and punish those accused of occult practices. This book argues that women are weaker in their flesh, and they contain carnal desires that far exceed those of men: "But the natural reason is that she is more carnal than a man, as is clear from her many carnal abominations."

The logic is head-spinning, but, according to the *Malleus Maleficarum*, because Eve in the Bible was created from Adam's rib, womankind is imperfect and "quicker to waver in her faith, and consequently quicker to abjure the faith, which is the root of witchcraft. This is presented as God's design, which makes it difficult to argue against.

Later in the *Malleus Maleficarum*, the type of women given to witchcraft are further defined, specifically as "adulterous drabs and whores." In other words, women who enjoy sex or who don't adhere to the patriarchal family system must be in league with the Devil. To further demonize women who dare step outside of their biblically defined roles, witches were described in the *Malleus Maleficarum* as stealing men's penises and hiding them.

During this time, European nation-states were racing to "discover" and colonize the area that they termed the *New World*, as if no one lived there already. At the same time that secular courts were beginning to take over witchcraft trials, inflation was ravaging European economies. The resources from the New World created a huge gap between the poor and wealthy merchants and monarchs. Overpopulation led to land shortages and hunger; economies fell into recessions and depressions; and the monarchies worked to centralize their powers by growing their militaries, levying ever higher taxes, and seizing publicly shared land. People were desperate and afraid, and most people believed in witchcraft.

These volatile conditions hurt everyone who wasn't part of the royal or upper classes—especially women, whose pay and opportunities were limited and dwindling. Witch accusations spun out from these class and economic concerns. Extremely poor or homeless individuals were vulnerable to accusations because they were viewed as a drain on resources. Accusations could be levied on a widow who owned prime real estate or a thriving business like a tavern or inn. Accusers could attack a politically powerful man by naming his wife and daughters.

One employment option open to sixteenth-century women was as the village healer. This role was akin to a lay physician, but during this period was often conflated with witchcraft. The position of healer became even more precarious as laws were adjusted to criminalize aspects of sexual relationships and birth. Men also began moving into the profession as medical training at universities developed. Women lacked access to institutional education.

While lay physicians were aiding and protecting their patients and creating a valuable inventory of herbal medicines, the powers that be viewed their work, especially as it related to the birthing process, with suspicion. In the *Malleus Maleficarum*, midwives were specifically called out because they have the opportunity to "commit [crimes] against infants, both in a mother's womb and afterwards." Only midwives and healers who were women are under suspicion; as "the Devils do these things through the medium of women, and not men, this form of homicide is associated rather with women than with men." These beliefs made it dangerous to be a local healer, and may have set the tone for persecutions that continue to

Michelle Proby

THE ROOTS OF THE SATANIC PANIC

I n the 1980s and '90s, parents were warned of the occult hidden everywhere: in the television shows their children watched, in games like Dungeons and Dragons (teaching the youth to do spells), and many, many other pop-culture touchstones. Much of this fear came from books and televangelists shouting warnings, but also from panicked headlines in tabloid media. Then there was the 1980 "memoir" *Michelle Remembers*, which detailed the abusive childhood of a woman named Michelle Proby at the hands of a satanic cult. It's important to note that nearly everything in this book has been debunked, and the so-called recovered-memory therapy that was used to get the details of Proby's story is highly criticized by those in the psychiatric community. Proby's story, though, made nearly every major news outlet and daytime talk show.

Proby's story is a difficult one to hear. It begins when she was twenty-seven years old and a patient of Dr. Lawrence Pazder, a psychiatrist specializing in intensive psychotherapy involving the highly controversial practice of "recovering" memories. In their sessions, Proby uncovered memories that she had been abused as a young child, first by her mother and then by a man named Malachi, the leader of a secret satanic cult. Malachi, she told Dr. Pazder, led his cult members in sexual rituals, and she was forced to both watch and participate. As she told the story, the details of the trauma got more specific and more gruesome. She told one particularly horrible story about being placed in a car with a dead body. Members of the cult then set the car on fire; she remembered the hospital afterward, being treated for the burns. In another session, she recalled a cult-run operating room where they surgically implanted horns on her skull.

Like many stories told during recovered-memory therapy sessions, these were not true. Memory, as science tells us, is a malleable thing, and these memories simply never happened. But the fallout from Dr. Pazder's sessions with Michelle Proby still caused widespread damage. In 1980, he published *Michelle Remembers*, detailing Proby's story (using the name Michelle Smith to maintain some anonymity). The book was an immediate best seller, kicking off a hysteria that spread across the United States of America like wildfire. It was seen as published proof that satanic cults did exist—and that they were out doing active harm to the youth of America.

The fear that satanic cults were sacrificing the innocent reached a fever pitch in the summer of 1983 when Judy Johnson, the mother of a young student at the McMartin preschool, filed a police report in Manhattan Beach, California, alleging that school employee Ray Buckey had abused her son and others. A team of psychiatrists and other medical professionals were brought in to interview two hundred children who had attended the school at one time or another. After being subject to interview techniques that are now considered inappropriate (like leading questions), hundreds of children said that they were abused physically and sexually while at the preschool. Johnson continued to call the police, giving more and more fantastic stories, including saying that the teachers dressed as witches, that they sacrificed animals, and that they forced her son to drink blood from a baby. When the trial went to court in 1984, it was a media sensation. Other accusations began to fly across the country, and supposed secret satanic child sex rings were being "discovered" across several states. The panic set in. The children were in danger.

It's easy to dismiss what happened as a kind of anomaly in recent US history. After all, much of what we remember about the Satanic Panic today is almost funny—like people worrying that the Smurfs were teaching young children about the occult. The idea is patently absurd. But real lives were uprooted in the trials that ensued. And the entire panic says multitudes about the culture's views of women's place in society. Just as women were entering the workplace in record numbers, suddenly the children were at risk. The messaging was clear: if a mother wanted to keep her children safe, then she needed to make sure that she was at home to keep an eye on them. It was echoed every night, with news stations blasting, "It's ten p.m. Do you know where your children are?"

These anxieties surrounding the safety of children do not flare when men are the ones in the office. But in the 1980s, when women were outside of the home, suddenly it seemed as if the children were at risk. Not only were they in danger, but the supposed danger was heightened with occult connections. The allegations were never solely of abuse, unfortunately a very real problem, but they were accusations of satanic abuse, blood rituals, and witchcraft that stand out— as if women leaving the home is going against every godly tenet.

While the Satanic Panic had real and devastating consequences in North America, especially for the people who found themselves under investigation for satanic ritual abuse in cases like the McMartin preschool trial, the idea that satanic symbols lurked everywhere has since become a thing of mockery. After all, it can be hard to believe that people would find something as innocent as Saturday morning cartoons evil. But the panic was real.

Proby is considered the first match that lit the flame—but in a way she, too, was a victim of the nascent panic. Proby went on to marry Dr. Pazder, the psychiatrist who oversaw her therapy and published her sensational story. She didn't comment much on her past history, though as decades went on and Pazder's therapy techniques were subject to more scrutiny and criticism, the doctor did admit that some of the details may have been fabricated or implanted through suggestion. It's not clear whether Proby herself believed her story or not, though people who "recover" false memories often do believe very sincerely in their confabulations. What is certain, though, is that these kinds of extreme stories can quickly turn conspiratorial, if not kept in check. And, as we know, conspiracies can spread like a wildfire, and be just as destructive.

D&D: THE "DEVIL'S GAME" WELCOME WOMEN

During the Satanic Panic of the 1980s and '90s, parents were warned that tabletop games like Dungeons and Dragons would turn their children into little witches and warlocks, acting as a kind of occult gateway to all sorts of sordid activities. In fact, maybe no game (save for the Ouija board) was deemed as devilish and dangerous as Dungeons and Dragons. The game, which was designed by Gary Gygax and Dave Arneson, first hit the market in 1974. The popularity of the game survived the negative press of the 1980s moral panic, however, as adolescents everywhere gathered to play the game. Adolescent boys, that is. While girls were not specifically excluded, the game got the reputation for being a "boys' game," at least in popular culture. This was not intentional, but perhaps an unintentional side effect of the moral panic. In 2000, the TV show *Freaks and Geeks* would show a group of boys playing in an episode. Rivers Cuomo, the front man for the band Weezer, would sing about playing "In the Garage." In more recent years, Netflix's show *Stranger Things* is built around four boys who are equipped with special knowledge of how to take down monsters gleaned from hours upon hours of playing D&D in their basement. Pop culture rarely showed groups of girls playing with the same kind of intensity.

In 2017, publisher Wizards of the Coast reported that Dungeons and Dragons had the highest number of players in its history. More people than ever were playing the game that was once deemed occult. Even better, 40 percent of those playing were women. Part of that shift was enabled by decisions made by the gaming company, who hired more women as artists and directors. Women like Kate Welch, Shauna Narciso, and Kate Irwin helped make the game more inclusive. Previously, benefits and weaknesses were assigned to characters based on gender. A female character, for instance, would have a strength disadvantage compared to her male counterpart. But now, gender doesn't play a role in character creation. As the fifth edition of the *Player's Handbook* says, players are encouraged to think beyond "binary notions of sex and gender." Gone are also the gendered clothes that female characters were often drawn wearing, like fur bikinis. In a 2018 interview with the *Mary Sue*, Irwin said that these clothing choices were about equality but also about making the game more realistic: "Would a wizard really wear super heavy robes going through a swamp? Wouldn't that hinder them as they're doing things?" In other words, most warriors are not going to do their best fighting in a bikini.

In the end, it is fascinating to see how society has progressed by looking through the lens of the occult-adjacent game of Dungeons and Dragons. What began as a world largely focused on the male gaze has become something working toward inclusivity.

Eleanor "Nora" Sidgwick

FIRST FEMALE MEMBER OF THE PSYCHICAL SOCIETY

Throughout Western history, there has been a gender split inside occult circles, just like the one that exists outside of those communities. Back in the sixteenth and seventeenth centuries, men could be sorcerers, magicians, and alchemists associated with royal courts and aristocracy, with institutional support and even the veneer of scientific validity, while women were marginalized (and sometimes endangered) by the label *witch*. During Spiritualism's heyday, the majority of practitioners were women. It makes a kind of unfortunate sense, then, that when scientists and amateur philosophers began investigating and debunking mediums and psychics, the majority of these clubs and psychical societies would be made up of men. For instance, while the British Ghost Club did welcome women as members as it approached the twentieth century, it quite likely began in 1862 as an exclusively gentlemen's club.

This gender split is echoed in Spiritualism; women are vessels (as the spirit's physical connection to Earth), and as powerful as that role is, they can ultimately lose control of the narrative as they are usually channeling a male spirit's voice. These women often had their own ideas, but they needed the male voice to validate them. Even so, men's ideas seem to be emphasized while women took a more passive role. More than that, even when women embraced the occult and had a captive audience willing to listen to the voices they channeled, they could be silenced and denounced as frauds by male investigators. When men step into the occult space, they are afforded more authority and respect, even more control over what qualifies as real, whether they are acting as an investigator or a magician.

But not all of the debunkers and skeptics were men. Beginning in the late nineteenth century, women also joined this investigation of practitioners of the occult. These women were investigating mediums not to persecute them but rather to protect their vulnerable and grieving clients from fraud. They used scientific methods of their time to learn if communication with the dead really was possible. We can see these women's concerns and questions as setting the stage for current conversations about ethical questions in the occult.

The push to investigate mediums took off in the nineteenth century, right on the heels of the founding of Spiritualism. In 1882, Henry Sidgwick, a faculty member of Trinity College, Cambridge, and two of his friends, Frederic Myers and Edmund Gurney, organized the British Society for Psychical Research. These men, particularly Gurney, pulled Harvard psychologist William James, brother of writer Henry James, into the fold. Professor James then brought the idea across the pond, helping to found the American Society for Psychical Research in 1884.

The Psychical Societies would become home bases of sorts for scientists and academics to pursue investigations into paranormal phenomena, especially the work of mediums. Some of the best-known investigators and debunkers of psychics would include scientists and psychologists like Michael Faraday and William James, truth seekers like Richard Hodgson, and stage magicians like Harry Houdini (and, much later, James Randi)—but the ranks of skeptics over the years haven't only included men. The mathematician Eleanor "Nora" Balfour Sidgwick, the wife of founder Henry Sidgwick, was involved in the British Society for Psychical Research from its start. Eventually, she served as one of its presidents, and she was the organization's honorary secretary for almost a quarter of a century.

Sidgwick and her husband were supporters of higher education for women, and her career outside of the Society for Psychical Research, or SPR, was spent in the administration of Newnham College of the University of Cambridge. In addition to her skills in mathematics, she was educated in English literature and several languages. She grew up in the Balfour family, which counted several politicians and scientists in its number.

Her interest in the paranormal was aroused in the 1870s when she, her brother Arthur Balfour, and friends, including Henry, sat with numerous mediums. The result of these sittings was twofold: she developed a curiosity about communication between the living and the dead and an intense concern about the fraud they witnessed.

Sidgwick collaborated on numerous projects of the SPR. She helped compile the 1886 book by Frederic Myers and Edmund Gurney *Phantasms of the Living*. This was a compendium of what the authors believed to be evidence of apparitions conjured through thought transference, or telepathy. Sidgwick later condensed the book into one volume. She also performed her own investigations into witnesses' stories of hauntings, and meticulously culled the ones that she felt could have been the result of hallucinations; this angered some members who felt that she was *too* skeptical. (In her 2007 book *Ghost Hunters*, journalist Deborah Blum notes that Sidgwick was unruffled by these criticisms, to her husband's delight.) One common thread that made her question the reality of ghosts was that ghosts wore clothes, even though they were spirits. This seemed impossible, and she concluded that instead of investigating ghosts, perhaps they should be investigating why so many people believed they had seen them.

Additionally, Sidgwick played a role in investigations of mediums, such as Leonora Piper (whom we met in chapter 3). According to historian Alan Gauld, Sidgwick produced a 657-page-long study about Piper's trances in 1915. Evidently, she and her husband, like other unsatisfied sitters, found several of Piper's controls unconvincing, and she suggested that Piper was in a kind of hypnotic trance that allowed her to experience telepathy with her sitters, thus leading her occasionally to hit on details the sitters believed Piper couldn't know. This speculation was consistent with theories of the SPR. Many members wondered if paranormal activity could be related to telepathy instead of supernatural communication with spirits, an idea that anticipated theories of extrasensory perception to come.

Interestingly, while the members of the SPR strove to achieve a balanced view of the occult and use scientific principles to study the paranormal, they constantly irritated each of their constituencies. On the one hand, these investigations into supernatural matters during a moment of industrial and scientific progress, as well as debates over the new theory of evolution, led to criticism of the group from scientists who felt that investigating the paranormal was a waste of time. On the other hand, the society's record of disproving the powers of mediums during investigations angered believers like Arthur Conan Doyle, who resigned his membership. Doyle thought that the members of the society were too skeptical of spirit communication and would never be open to the possibility of the supernatural. But for someone as meticulous as Sidgwick, a healthy dose of skepticism wasn't a bias; it was a part of the job.

Amy E. Tanner

T hat Amy E. Tanner earned a PhD in philosophy (magna cum laude) from the University of Chicago in 1898 is impressive; though the majority of universities were open to women by that time, it was still unusual for a woman to pursue a doctorate, let alone achieve one. Beyond that, she was a successful researcher in a discipline not friendly to women participants. But once Tanner had her degree and had begun her accomplished research career, job prospects still did not materialize. She may have had a degree, but that didn't mean she would be hired over a male candidate for an academic position. She remained at Chicago as an associate researcher for four years and then taught at Wilson College. In 1904, she wrote an influential book—*The Child: His Thinking, Feeling, and Doing*—that played a role in the decision of eminent psychology professor G. Stanley Hall to hire her at Clark University.

In her research, which often combined philosophy and psychology, Tanner did not shy away from topics and debates related to gender. She may have published her book on child psychology, but her other projects seemed affected by her situation as a woman trying to negotiate the patriarchal world of universities. At Wilson in the early 1900s, she pursued an ethnographic study of waitressing by becoming one and writing about the experience. Like much of her work, this led her to consider the politics of labor reform, and ultimately to support the work of labor unions and their push for a shorter work day.

In addition to her thoughts on labor reform gleaned from her research, Tanner weighed in on the debates over women's intelligence that were percolating at the time. In 1891, Joseph Jastrow made a study of his undergraduate students, men and women, and asserted that his results supported the theory that women had inferior "mental variability," because they could not produce as varied and lengthy lists of words as his male students. Tanner responded to this in an article in the *Psychological Review* in 1896, writing: "The real tendencies of women cannot be known until they are free to choose, any more than those of a tied-up dog can be." She suggested that limitations in education and social opportunities for women made objective gendered tests of intelligence unreliable, to say the least.

While at Wilson College pursuing her research projects, Tanner wrote to G. Stanley Hall, the president of Clark University in Massachusetts. She wondered if there could be a position for her at Clark. In her letter to Hall, she wrote, "I have reached the maximum salary here and have developed my work as far as the size of the college will justify," and observed, "One is truly unfortunate, from a financial standpoint, to be a woman with a love of philosophizing!" Aware of her publication record in the field, Hall hired Tanner as an honorary university fellow. Although she became the head of experimental pedagogy for Clark University's Children's Institute in 1909, she never achieved tenured faculty status, leading her to leave academia in 1918. Hall noted in a letter when Tanner resigned her lectureship that "she was (with too much ground, alas) dissatisfied that women are not recognized in the university." When she left Clark University in 1918, she purchased, and thereafter managed, the Majestic Cinema in Worcester, Massachusetts.

"The real tendencies of
women cannot be known
until they are free to choose,
any more than those of a
tied-up dog can be."

—Amy E. Tanner

It's not surprising that Tanner's attention turned to mediums and psychic activity. The connection of women to Spiritualism, and the religion's hold on a public desperately seeking answers, would have made it a prime target of investigation for a woman with a PhD in the social sciences. In her preface to *Studies in Spiritism*, her 1910 book about experiments that she and Hall conducted with medium Leonora Piper, she showed an awareness of the popularity of mediumship, noting, "now seems to be the psychological moment to present the reverse side of the case of Spiritism." Even with this explicit goal of presenting the "reverse side," she asserted an open and inquiring mind—but after her experiments with Hall, she found no evidence of these phenomena, and she questioned the results of studies completed by the Psychical Societies. She and Hall wanted to approach their investigation without any preconceived notions. She believed that previous researchers, the majority of them men, had been too accepting of Piper's "controls," or spirit guides, as valid supernatural phenomena, thus throwing off any results they thought they achieved. Those researchers found precisely what they were looking for.

Investigator Richard Hodgson, as we learned in the last chapter, was one of those researchers who found what he wanted to find; he expressed the belief that Piper could be in genuine contact with the "other side." After Hodgson died in 1905, Piper (rather cheekily) started claiming that he was her new control. Tanner and Hall had serious doubts. The Hodgson control had memories of a close friendship between the living Hodgson and Hall that never existed. Furthermore, the Hodgson control believed the fictional narratives and characters that Hall and Tanner fed him. The Hodgson control even went so far as to bring a fictitious niece Hall and Tanner had created, Bessie Beals, to speak with Hall. Hall wrote, "As to the identity of

Hodgson, the so-called control, he surely was not all there, and what was present of him, if anything, was not only fragmentary but incredibly stupid, oblivious, and changed." Rather than accepting the control, as some Psychical Society members had, Hall and Tanner questioned "Hodgson," challenged him, tricked him, and withheld information when he went fishing for it. Hall was not impressed, and he and Tanner chalked up Piper's controls to a case of secondary personality.

Tanner expanded on this diagnosis in chapter 19 of *Studies in Spiritism*, "Theory of the Piper Case." She outlined several explanations for Piper's trance mediumship that were consistent with psychological theories of that time, and none of them were supernormal. Both Hall and Tanner interpreted Piper's controls during her trances as "secondary personalities," or weaker parts of a larger personality that, Tanner explained using Freudian theories, would break off in times of trauma. Tanner noted that Piper's trances increased and her controls became more coherent near times that she experienced shocks. The first shock was a sledding accident when Piper was sixteen years old that left her severely injured; later shocks Tanner noted included surgeries for tumors in her reproductive organs and for a hernia. Piper's trances seemed suspicious to Tanner as well because she never fell into one involuntarily. By Piper's own account, she only went into trances when she was sitting for people.

Hall and Tanner questioned and tested Piper's controls to a degree that, at least to Tanner's knowledge, no experimenter had done before. Piper's entire career as a medium had been championed and supported by Spiritualists and researchers. Her controls were accepted as spirits without question. Tanner noted that sitters would help explain incomplete or incorrect messages from controls to try to create a coherent narrative out of the automatic writing. (Automatic writing was Piper's preferred method of spirit communication; she used a pencil and paper to scrawl messages from her control during trances.) Indeed, Tanner asserted that the controls fished for clues from sitters frequently during their study and in written accounts of sittings. "The very life of the control," she concluded, "seems to depend on his being stimulated by questions and suggestions." In the same vein, Tanner believed that without constant framing, even unconsciously, by sitters eager for information and by Piper's managers, who would offer explanations for sitters during sessions or identify new spirits in the room, the control would fall silent or become incomprehensible. Finally, Tanner pointed to Piper's own evident belief in her powers and her personality. Tanner suggested that most mediums, Piper included, were highly impressionable and open to receiving visions and omens. She believed that individuals who were primed to believe in spirits would have no trouble entering trance states or dissociating their minds and personalities.

Interestingly, although Tanner debunked Piper and identified the weaknesses in the psychical societies' methods, she approached Piper in a more human way than previous researchers had. Both Hall and Hodgson dismissed Piper's input and gave no thought to her condition during the experiments. When asked about Piper's curiosity about what caused her trances, Hodgson said, "Mrs. Piper's opinion, in any case, is of no value." By contrast, Tanner emphasized Piper's isolation from her neighbors and church and thought that she had been exhausted and further isolated by her work with the psychical societies. Perhaps she had empathy for Piper's position as a woman, and understood that mediums were finding a way to achieve some power in a misogynistic society. But her own power came from her skeptical investigations.

THE SCULLY EFFECT

The *X-Files* was a cultural touchstone in the 1990s, and its appeal continues today. In addition to its nine original seasons that began in 1993, it spawned two movies and two additional seasons in 2016 and 2018, respectively. Most Americans, even if they didn't watch the show, recognize the names of the main characters, the theme song, and the show's slogan, "The Truth Is Out There."

Protagonists Fox Mulder and Dana Scully, played by David Duchovny and Gillian Anderson, are FBI agents who investigate possible supernatural threats—ranging from cults and cryptids to vast government conspiracies about alien contact. This is part of a long tradition of occult detective narratives going back to the nineteenth century, stories that involve scientific or rational investigation of paranormal events or creatures. *The X-Files* also became a transition point in television media from shows like Rod Serling's *The Twilight Zone* (1959–1964), Jeffrey Grant Rice's *Kolchak: The Night Stalker* (1974–1975), and David Lynch's *Twin Peaks* (1990–1991) to the explosion of horror and paranormal shows of the late 1990s through today. The show developed narrative techniques still common in TV: overarching plots carrying through multiple weeks or seasons, alongside the more traditional procedural "monster of the week" episode format.

There is another piece to the legacy of *The X-Files*, though, and it moves beyond the screen to the real world: the Scully Effect. Many young women who watched the show when it aired were inspired by the character of Agent Dana Scully to enter STEM fields. Rather than simply being a sidekick of Mulder, Scully was an equal partner in the investigations. Moreover, she was the rational and scientific medical doctor of the show, a female character practically unseen on television screens in the 1990s. Scully also played the role of the skeptic in contrast to Mulder's identity as a hard-core believer in paranormal phenomena. This pairing flies in the face of the tendency in paranormal shows to cast women as believers and men as skeptics that we discussed in our last chapter.

In 2018, the Geena Davis Institute on Gender in Media completed a survey of over 2,000 American women over age 25, the majority of whom watched *The X-Files* and half of whom were in STEM fields. The institute reported a significant overlap in the numbers of women who pursued careers in STEM fields and watched the show. This study appeared to corroborate the anecdotal evidence reported previously by women who entered STEM fields and were fans of the show.

Rose Mackenberg

R ose Mackenberg was a private detective adept at disguises, handpicked by Harry Houdini for his "Secret Service"—an elite group of investigators who traveled the country ahead of his show dates to collect research about mediums so that Houdini could expose them upon his arrival. However, Mackenberg continued to be the bane of mediums in the United States on her own after Houdini passed away in 1926. In a March 3, 1951, article for the *Saturday Evening Post*, she told Joseph Fulling Fishman that, at that point in time, she had been "a professional investigator of Spiritualistic mediums" for almost thirty years. Like Tanner before her, she believed grief to be the reason most people sought out messages from beyond. Mackenberg went further, however, and predicted that the number of mediums would grow the longer the US remained at war. In telling her story to Fishman, Mackenberg was careful to insist that she respected Spiritualism as a religion, and while she never found a real medium in her investigations, she left the door open to whether any true psychics actually existed.

Mackenberg met Houdini during her work as a private detective. When a case she had taken on for a bank employee required her to investigate a medium, she went to Houdini for advice. After helping her with her case, he recruited her for his team and trained her in the art of catching fraudulent mediums. She was an eager and quick study. That 1951 *Saturday Evening Post* article included photographs of Mackenberg demonstrating how mediums ply their trade with tricks like levitating a trumpet and table tilting. She supplemented her investigation gigs with lectures and demonstrations of the psychic tricks of the trade, carrying on the work of Houdini and his Secret Service.

It makes sense that Houdini would employ Mackenberg to help him expose frauds, since both of them saw fraudulent mediums as predators exploiting their prey's grief. From a young age, Houdini had been curious about Spiritualism and mediums, and he was always disappointed. This even damaged his friendship with Arthur Conan Doyle, whose wife sometimes led séances. When Houdini sat with Doyle's wife, she claimed she had contacted Houdini's mother. According to Houdini biographers William Kalush and Larry Sloman, Houdini denied the "spirit" was his mother, citing numerous inconsistencies, including the spirit's "torrent of sappy words in perfect English." Houdini also knew from coded messages from his wife, Bess, that Lady Doyle had asked her many questions about Houdini's mother the previous evening.

Ever the showman, Houdini decided to market debunking mediums as a part of his act. In addition to his escape spectacles, he offered prizes, wagers, and challenges to mediums in towns on his circuit. The resulting publicity drew large audiences, sometimes even resulting in riots in the theater. He quickly realized that

he couldn't do it all alone. He would expose frauds in his stage show, but he needed assistants to gather the necessary intel. These assistants would become what Kalush and Sloman call "a whole combat division." This was Houdini's Secret Service.

Houdini recruited women to his Secret Service group, like his showgirls, his niece Julia Sawyer, and Mackenberg, because they could pose as easy marks suffering from grief—or, as Mackenberg said in her conversation with Fishman, they could put on a "dumb act" and string mediums along, getting more information. Disguising herself as a widow, a schoolteacher, or a woman just in from the country curious about the spirits, Mackenberg could manipulate the mediums' expectations and make herself look less threatening and more enticing to a fake. Journalist Gavin Edwards noted that she also used aliases that often subtly, or not so subtly, poked fun at her own marks, names like Francis Raud, F. Raud, or Allicia Bunck.

While the names and the disguises make her work sound like exciting fodder for an escapist television show, Mackenberg didn't shy away from sharing a little about the dark side of being a woman investigating mediums. Mackenberg told Fishman about incidents in which she had to trip or slap male psychics and run, had her clothes torn while escaping, or had to bust through a locked door to get out of a bad situation. She concluded, "Fortunately, I am a fairly strong woman and have been able to defend myself. Several times, after I had related such experiences to Houdini, he suggested that I carry a gun. But I never could bring myself to do it."

Susan Gerbic

LEADER OF THE GUERILLA SKEPTICS

There's no business quite like the psychic business. According to Jack Hitt in his 2019 *New York Times* article "Inside the Secret Sting Operation to Expose Celebrity Psychics," in 2018, there were approximately 95,000 "psychic businesses" in the US, leading to a revenue of almost $2 billion. Talking to the dead for paying customers can be a lucrative pursuit. As long as there have been individuals who believed they could communicate with spirits and charged for the service, there have been others who have questioned the very possibility of spirit communication. Whether they think psychics are frauds or simply misguided believers, skeptics pursue what they perceive as the path of truth and try to protect unwitting marks from deception and financial loss.

One of these skeptics working today is Susan Gerbic. Based in California, Gerbic is a former photographer who, before retirement, managed a J. C. Penney portrait studio. Now, she heads up a group of "guerilla" online skeptics committed to debunking celebrity mediums, or "grief vampires," as Gerbic and her partner Mark Edward call them. As outlined by Hitt in his *New York Times* piece, Gerbic, her collaborator Edward (a performing mentalist and magician), and the rest of her Guerilla Skeptics group use social media to trip up psychics who spice up the traditional cold reading with a little research.

"The stage psychics, those who claim to communicate with the dead, are my specialty. We call them grief vampires. And this is my prediction: their days are numbered."

—Susan Gerbic

In the psychic world, there are a couple ways to know things about people without any communication with spirits from beyond. One of these methods is a cold reading, which involves close observation of a subject's clothes, mannerisms, and body language. Once a psychic begins to offer guesses, suggestions, and leading statements, they can gauge the subject's reactions. Of course, having one or two facts about a subject before a reading can help with credibility and to move things along, and this is known as a hot reading. Research into their clients' families, professions, and losses has been a part of psychics' to-do lists for a long time. Back in the nineteenth and early twentieth centuries, psychic mediums could hire private investigators; they could do their own research at the cemetery and library; or they could glean information from newspapers regarding social events, marriages, births, or deaths. At times, they even shared tidbits of information with their colleagues through gossip or from rumored apocryphal "blue books." One of the easiest methods was to plant assistants who could eavesdrop on waiting clients and report what they learned to the medium. Twenty-first-century psychics can do these things as well. In fact, they do plant staff among the waiting audience and, at times, use wires so an assistant can feed them information while they are onstage. But they have a big advantage over the turn-of-the-century mediums: they can just jump on the internet, which has a global reach. Today, many audience members respond to Facebook event invitations, so it's easy for mediums or their researchers to identify promising Facebook profiles for perusal.

With this temptation to research on social media in mind, Gerbic and her team create what Hitt calls "Facebook sock puppets." These are fake profiles that are curated for a long enough time and with realistic enough content to create believable personas, which the team members can then use as their identities when they attend psychic events. If mediums have done their Facebook preshow homework well, the persona becomes a tempting target.

When Gerbic and her team identify a medium and attend an event to collect evidence, she assigns the mission a name such as "Operation Bumblebee" or "Operation Pizza Roll" and leaves calling cards with the name at the event. Gerbic explained to Hitt that the names are all "easy to spell and easy to remember. So even if you throw the card away, you might remember 'Operation Pizza Roll.' And you'll say, You know what, I've got a couple of minutes before the show starts; I'm going to see what this Operation Tater Tot is all about." When the audience members search for the operation on their phone, they can discover information about the medium provided by Gerbic and her team, and, she hopes, take this into consideration as they make up their own minds. Gerbic and her team have tangled with several psychics, including Sylvia Browne, Thomas John, and Chip Coffey, to name a few.

Outreach is important for Gerbic to allow people to see another side to the psychic reading experience. She writes up reports of her group's sting operations for her regular column for *Skeptical Inquirer,* "Guerilla Skepticism," and she and Edward have been guests on several podcasts, including the *Oh No, Ross and Carrie* podcast (which investigates a range of fringe groups and pseudoscience). In their most recent guest appearance, from October 2021, they described their investigations of psychic Thomas John and his readings both onstage and in his 2018 Lifetime television show *Seatbelt Psychic.* They also explained how psychics have shifted their readings to Zoom as a result of the pandemic, leading to new adaptations of old cold and hot reading tricks. Even with these changes in the format of the readings, the Guerilla Skeptics continue to investigate how the psychic performance is constructed for and sold to audiences.

The history of the occult is a pendulum. For every time our culture sees women gaining power—fame, fortune, influence, independence—we see a period of reckoning. When women derive their power from mundane sources, like Rebecca Nurse owning disputed property or wives in the 1980s going to work, the backlash often comes in the form of accusations about Satanism or witchcraft. When they derive their power from the occult, the criticism may come from hardline rationalists. It's the opposition that's the point.

Sometimes, this is pure misogyny at work. At other times, opposition to the occult comes from curiosity. Women like Susan Gerbic, Amy Tanner, Rose Mackenberg, and Eleanor Sidgwick all took part in investigating these claims of the occult and the paranormal, alongside male investigators. If earlier ghost-hunting societies excluded women, then these women were working to legitimize gender equality in the investigative space. Sometimes the place of opposition can be a place of power in its own way.

In a way, these women are an important part of keeping the occult world both equal and ethical. As we've seen with the Salem witch trials and the Satanic Panic, however, it's not always such a simple journey to follow. Anti-occultism can be sinister. At its worst, it is used as a tool to disempower women and persecute those who don't neatly fit society's standards. Challengers to the occult, whatever their reasons, are important foils for the next group of women we'll meet: the ones who, even in the face of detractors, choose to own their occult identity wholly and without apology. A large segment of today's occult community is about exploding gender binaries, looking to include science to the spiritual, and ensuring that ethical practices include everyone who wants to join—and that no one is hurt along the way.

5

100% THAT WITCH

EMBRACING THE OCCULT

Tituba was one of the first women in Salem who admitted to participating in the witchcraft activities of which she was accused. In her testimony, she wove fantastical stories of meeting with the Devil and seeing supernatural occurrences under the cover of night. Her stories lent validity to the townspeople's suspicions—but that doesn't mean they were true. Tituba most likely accepted the label of *witch* because, as an enslaved person, she couldn't accuse a white man of lying. Doing so would've been devastating, even life-threatening, to her. She never would have known it, but in a way, Tituba anticipated the pendulum swing of women and the occult.

Women's relationship to the occult isn't—and has never been—a stable one. At times, the occult is embraced by mainstream society (as seen with the rise of Spiritualism). During these upswings, women can gain social power and economic stability by participating in the occult. But, as we've noted many times in this book, the culture is not always willing to accept the paranormal. And this is where Tituba is so important. She was an enslaved Black woman trying to live in a white, patriarchal, and Christian society that believed in satanic witchcraft. Tituba's only defense of her very life was to confess to being a witch, whether she practiced any aspect of what Puritans called the occult or not. She reminds us of the danger of a culture that rejects women and people of color. A strictly patriarchal culture leaves women powerless, and in order to maintain that power structure, it invents accusations to keep women at the bottom.

The good news is that we refuse to stay there. And one of the ways we can regain power is by voluntarily doing what Tituba did out of necessity: embracing the accusation instead of running away. Sometimes the most powerful response to an attack is "yeah, I am—so what?"

We've seen throughout this book that the occult is a way for women to gain power in places that society generally won't allow them, whether that be in the political, religious, or domestic realm. But a powerful woman can be a dangerous thing—and there has been a backlash to the occult time and time again to prove it. And often, the women under attack will fight back by saying, "Yes. I am a powerful woman"—even if that means also saying, "Yes, I am a witch." Simply owning an identity is a power play in and of itself.

Take *Bewitched*, the popular 1960s sitcom in which Elizabeth Montgomery played a witch housewife, Samantha Stephens. When *Bewitched* appeared on American airwaves in 1964, it initially seemed to be a callback to earlier family sitcoms like *The Donna Reed Show*, but it subverted domesticity in its own way. For one thing, the Stephenses shared a double bed, unlike previous sitcom couples. By emphasizing Samantha's powers and including slight threads of protest with the running argument that humans and witches aren't that different after all, *Bewitched* seemed to try to question the conformity and oppression that remained from the 1950s in a show that bridged the 1960s and 1970s. Even though Samantha appears to try to ignore her powers in favor of a more "normal" life, she ultimately is a witch—a label she wears proudly.

To see that pride in action, look no further than the other women who performed the witch in popular culture. Maila Nurmi, best known as her horror host character Vampira, flouted 1950s expectations of women—the perfect housewife, taking care of her home while looking picture-perfect—by becoming an exaggerated gothic subversion of the stereotype. She played the part of the ideal wife, ready to greet her husband at the door with a cocktail in hand. But the drink just might be his last, as she would playfully present a "poisoned" martini with an eyeball instead of an olive. Even her body, with her infamously small waistline, satirized the impossible body standards that diet culture presented to women. Decades later, Cassandra Peterson paid homage to Vampira when she donned her famous Elvira costume. The similarities between the two women make sense, given that the conservatism of the 1980s closely mirrored that of the '50s. Once again, family values were paramount, and women were encouraged to stay at home so that they could be "good" mothers. While Vampira played into the "housewife from hell" narrative, Elvira exploded it. She was a brazenly single, ambitious career woman who was unabashedly sexual. Elvira caused a scandal everywhere she went, with her low-cut goth dress and sexually charged jokes. Like Vampira, Elvira was a performance in satire, skewering the tightly wound conservative values of the day.

"Playing witch" was a form of public rebellion, of course, but there were also women working in their everyday lives to change public perception of women, using the occult as a label to indicate a kind of female power. Some women, like Louise Huebner (also known as "The Witch of Los Angeles"), used the witch label to attract a large following of admirers (and more than a little bit of controversy). Some women, though, used their standing in the occult community to affect real and tangible change in the world around them. Real-life practicing witch Laurie Cabot started the Witches' League for Public Awareness in the 1980s, a group working for civil liberties for those in the occult community.

In the last decades of the twentieth century, occult communities found themselves under attack during the Satanic Panic, a time when mainstream society embraced conservative values and saw the Devil in nearly every detail. It became dangerous to be different, as seen with the case of Brandi Blackbear, a high school student who was suspended and accused of practicing witchcraft. It sounds like the beginnings of the Salem witch trials, only set in much more recent history. Thankfully, we have had people willing to stand up in both the court of public opinion and in the legal court system to fight to ensure everyone has equal rights.

This long history of women enduring through the culture's swings from conservative to accepting and back again has paved the way for today's occult renaissance. Today, we are seeing women, men, and nonbinary individuals use their occult lifestyle to expand identity, especially to widen people's understanding of the full spectrum of what an identity can be. An excellent example is Krysta Venora, an "Afro-Indigenous, Trans, Non-Binary Queer, psychic witch, and spiritual counselor" by their own description, whose internet witchcraft is changing perceptions of who can be a leading voice in religion and spiritual practices. The practice of the occult is also a form of social resistance, revisiting history and expanding it beyond a white and Western lens. Alice Sparkly Kat's work on postcolonial astrology is a good example of how the current discussion around the occult is changing those long-held narratives. Similarly, women like Rachel True and Bri Luna are using their own craft to break down the hierarchies that have existed in the occult world for centuries.

Every person you'll see in this chapter, sometimes under dire circumstances, chose to find or regain some power by embracing the occult as part of themselves.

Tituba

The history of women and the occult in America begins with the 1692 Salem witch trials, which followed the larger European tradition of killing accused witches. As we saw in the last chapter, mostly (though not exclusively) white women were accused, and most of the time, these women were already marginalized in some way. At the start of the hysteria, there was one woman who was different from the other accused, and she unknowingly would set a trend for centuries of witches to come. Her name was Tituba.

Tituba was an enslaved person, owned by the Reverend Samuel Parris. She most likely lived in the Parris home, perhaps even sleeping next to the children, whom she helped raise and was reportedly close to. The Parris household would become important to the trials, as the reverend's daughter and niece were both accusers, and they both experienced "convulsions" at the invisible hands of the witches. Tituba was most likely from the Caribbean since that is where Parris brought her to Salem from, but ultimately, her place of birth is unknown. Trial records call her, at times, African; at other times she's described as an Indian. However she is described, it is clear that she is not white. Tituba is the Other that stands among the white citizens of Salem.

Tituba's otherness is an important detail. When she stood in front of the village of Salem to answer the charges of witchcraft that were burning like a fire through the community, she simply admitted to it all. Tituba had never been in trouble before. She was well-liked, and she was attached to the girls she cared for—and none of the girls who stayed with her accused her of any witchcraft. But when she was interrogated by John Hathorne in court about who tortured the girls, she said, "The devil, for all I know." She then began to weave a tale that would lead historian Stacy Schiff to refer to Tituba as a "sort of satanic Scheherazade," telling stories to save her life. Though she would never admit to hurting any children, she did say that she had been visited by the Devil, who came to her as an older man with white hair. She also claimed that she would "ride upon a stick or pole, and Good and Osborne behind me," and said that at one point the Devil caused her to go blind. Tituba's confession was quite unusual, both for the Salem trials and for the other trials that took place across Europe. Those accused of witchcraft almost always denied it, sometimes until their death, always holding true to their Christian ideals and beliefs.

So why did Tituba say that she was in league with Satan? Schiff, in her 2015 book *The Witches* on the Salem trials, explains that it was Tituba's otherness that made her confession necessary. Other people accused of witchcraft could prove their innocence and hopefully re-enter society as "changed" (i.e., reformed Christian) people. Tituba was never afforded that privilege. Even if she was found innocent of witchcraft, she would never be able to step back into society. Tituba was enslaved and, therefore, had no rights of her own. She knew what would happen if she accused a white person of lying. Tituba had no choice but cooperate. She spent fifteen months in prison, but the jury never indicted her. Why would they? She had no property to seize or money to confiscate. She couldn't leave prison without bond payment, something Reverend Parris refused to provide. Someone did pay it, though, and she was released. Tituba left Salem, and that's where her trail ends.

And so, she would go down in history as a Black African Indian witch, who taught voodoo to children and made deals with the Devil for her magic.

Tituba didn't intend for her lurid confession to make her a pop-culture figure—but in a way, it did. She's a central figure in Arthur Miller's play *The Crucible*, which uses the Salem trials as an allegory for Senator Joseph McCarthy's anti-communist "witch hunts." She also inspired her own fictionalized history, the 1986 French novel *I, Tituba, Black Witch of Salem* (as well as a 1964 middle-grade book called *Tituba of Salem Village*). In the not-especially-well-reviewed horror TV series *Salem* from the 2010s, she's a sexy Satan worshipper who embodies all the stories the real-life Tituba was pressured to tell about herself. And then there are all the other Black witches in pop culture, many of whom owe something to Tituba too. If the white witches of film and TV got to be the often-innocent white homemakers, then their Black counterparts had to deal with darker magic, which often left them nothing but unhappy memories.

In the 1936 film *Ouanga*, Klili (or Clelie), a Haitian woman who owns a plantation, uses voodoo to get revenge. She is a light-skinned Black woman in love with Adam, the white man who owns the plantation next to hers. When he chooses a white woman named Eve to marry instead of her, Klili uses her voodoo to send zombies to kidnap the bride-to-be so she can be sacrificed.

Early Hollywood horror and thriller films often used voodoo/hoodoo to construct an easy villain. An example is *White Zombie*, a 1932 film based on a William Seabrook novel. *White Zombie* stars Bela

Lugosi as a white Haitian man named Legendre who uses his voodoo powers (and army of zombies) to control a beautiful young woman named Madeleine, at the prompting of the wealthy plantation owner Charles. Madeleine is engaged to Neil, but Charles feels he must have her—at any cost. Lugosi, of course, is the villain, and the same "otherness" that gave him success with his portrayal of Dracula also succeeds here. Unfortunately, that means that white audiences saw his otherness, as well as the voodoo he used, as "evil." And Hollywood would continue to portray voodoo as an easy substitute for evil magic, even into the twenty-first century. To be clear, the words *voodoo* and *hoodoo* (at least as those terms are used in the United States, especially in places like New Orleans) are often used to describe practices that extended from Haitian Vodou, which is a religion, not mythology or folklore. It also is not evil in any way, despite what the depictions of zombies in the media have portrayed.

This exemplifies the problematic way in which Black witches (or truly, any nonwhite witches) have been viewed in pop culture, versus their white counterparts. While white witches have a long pedigree of both "good" and "bad" witches, they all are powerful, and the most popular of the bunch usually have a good heart. They are role models. Think Samantha from *Bewitched*: she's powerful, yes, but she's also a great wife and mom, and at the end of the day, she just wants her family to be happy. But Black witches aren't usually offered the same kind of diverse storytelling. Other examples of "voodoo" being used as shorthand for evil include the 1934 movie *Black Moon*, with Fay Wray fighting voodoo magic coming from native islanders in the Caribbean, and *I Walked with a Zombie* (from 1943) with white women once again in danger at the hands of "zombie" Black men who are being controlled by dark magic. It's a frustrating plot device that is used over and over again, for decades, continuing in later movies like 2005's *The Skeleton Key*, where two enslaved people called Mama Cecile and Papa Justify use voodoo to take over the bodies of a plantation owner's children, and *The Serpent and the Rainbow*, the 1988 Wes Craven film that puts Bill Pullman up against a Hatian bokor, a witch for hire. Being Black and being part of the occult is shorthand in these movies for evil magic that puts white protagonists in danger.

Today, as work by Black creatives claims its rightful space, the legacy of Tituba is stronger and more positive. Books like Tananarive Due's *The Good House* and films like *Eve's Bayou* present a more realistic view of Black women's relationship to the occult, and pop culture touchstones like Beyoncé's visual album *Lemonade* (which uses Yoruba imagery, including face makeup art by Brooklyn-based, Nigerian-born artist Laolu Senbanjo) are reclaiming the imagery of Black witchcraft and goddesses.

SALEM REIMAGINED

The events of Salem in 1692 have been revisited in national popular culture for centuries. Nineteenth-century writer Nathaniel Hawthorne was a descendant of Judge John Hathorne, who oversaw the inquiries and trials. Although Hathorne reserved his harshest judgment for the minister Cotton Mather in his 1835 story "Alice Doan's Appeal," his fiction, including the 1835 story "Young Goodman Brown" and the 1851 novel *The House of the Seven Gables*, was generally critical of what he saw as Puritanical hypocrisy. In 1953, Arthur Miller's play about the trials, *The Crucible*, brought the historical incident back to audiences' attention during another time of persecution, this one connected to the House Committee on Un-American Activities. In 1956, when Miller appeared before that committee, Shirley Jackson, a writer with her own ambiguous relationship to the occult, published a history book for children: *The Witchcraft of Salem Village*. Salem is often mentioned as a shorthand for persecution of various types, and the term *witch hunt* tends to be bandied about in times of political turmoil, as we've seen with former president Trump's impeachment trials. Salem still haunts our imaginations through contemporary fiction that directly references the witchcraft trials, such as the 2016 young adult novel *How to Hang a Witch* by Adriana Mather (a descendant of Cotton's) and *We Ride Upon Sticks* by Quan Barry from 2020.

In film, there is writer and director Robert Eggers's cinematic take on the horrors of 1600s Massachusetts in his 2015 period horror piece *The Witch*, starring Anya Taylor-Joy. Eggers's intense research into the time period, including speech patterns, vocabulary, literature, religious beliefs, and agriculture, creates a facsimile of the world of the New England colonists for the audience. But the movie, in its representation of witchcraft beliefs and accusations, mimics the stories and trial transcripts by making female independence and seduction the primary fears.

At the beginning of the movie, Thomasin, played by Taylor-Joy, and her family are banished to the wilderness, with all its evil connotations, because her father's spiritual beliefs don't quite match those of the Puritan leaders. Things quickly start to go downhill for them. The family falls into dissension fed by their own anxieties about trying to survive outside of the community, and witchcraft is a handy label to throw around. Thomasin prays anxiously for help controlling her impure thoughts, and her mother seems to worry about her teenage daughter's budding sexual awareness, eagerly desiring to enlist her in servitude with another family. Thomasin's siblings call her a witch to deflect attention away from their behavior, and her parents call her a witch when she questions their authority. Her father seems convinced she's diabolical only when she stands up to him and points out his inability to provide for the family. By the end of the movie, the implication is that there really are diabolical forces at work. Thomasin, the only survivor of the family, chooses to sign Satan's book after being promised fine clothes and travel. However, the gnawing thought on the part of the viewer remains that she is once again hemmed in by her lack of opportunities. She cannot live on her own in the wilderness or return to the Puritan town after the deaths of her family members. A woman alone in the seventeenth century in New England had few options, even in the movies.

Vampira

One of the biggest challenges in popular culture to 1950s society was an icon who, at times, muddled conceptions of performance and reality and destroyed midcentury conventions of home and family on late-night, local TV, all while emitting a blood-curdling scream.

That's right. We're talking about Vampira, and unlike other '50s housewives she wasn't into Tupperware parties—that is, unless they involved frothy potion cocktails with eyeball garnishes.

Vampira was the creation of Maila Elizabeth Syrjäniemi, a daughter of Finnish immigrants, who grew up feeling like she didn't fit in with her family or at school. This feeling of being an outcast seems to have led to a life-long pursuit of subverting the status quo. Her biographer W. Scott Poole writes that she had "a deep and abiding sympathy for challenges to the American consensus," and she "always understood herself as a freak, as weird, as problematic in relation to the wider culture."

When she first left home as a teen in the 1930s, she ended up doing a modeling gig in Los Angeles in 1940 before living for a short time in Greenwich Village. Somewhere in there, she changed her name to Maila Nurmi. An offer from Howard Hawks to be in a horror movie written by William Faulkner drew her back to Los Angeles, but the movie fell through.

During the 1940s, while she was picking up odd jobs in Los Angeles, she was drawn to underground movements like the Beats and made connections with counterculture individuals such as James Dean and Rudi Gernreich. Dean was the "rebel without a cause." Gernreich was a fashion designer who invented the thong and designed clothing that challenged traditionally accepted ideas about gender performance. He was a founding member of the Mattachine Society, an early group dedicated to the pursuit of LGBTQ+ rights in Los Angeles. Nurmi identified individuals like these as fellow nonconformists. She didn't fit in the contained, cookie-cutter 1950s American scene of the perfect housewife with a husband, kids, dog, and suburban home with a yard, and she didn't want to.

When she was younger, Nurmi had dreams of becoming a traveling evangelist called Sister Saint Francis. As this imagined character, Poole notes, she would "proclaim 'world peace,' perhaps put on display some 'psychic abilities,' and make boatloads of cash." She wanted to shock America into finally facing its reality hidden underneath the veneer of social conformity and the distraction of consumer culture. There was a lot of hidden horror in midcentury America, and not just because of the ever-present terror of large-scale nuclear brinkmanship.

There were unpleasant truths hidden beneath the slick surface presented on TV and in magazines. The movement of women back into the home and lack of opportunities outside of domestic spaces could lead to depression and anxiety and prescription medications. The romanticized TV version of the mid-twentieth century would have us believe that everyone and everything were middle-class and peaceful, but this was far from the case. Suburban homes could hide abuse, and violence in the home wasn't always frowned upon. It can be shocking for twenty-first-century audiences to view movies, TV shows, and advertisements from the time period and see men spanking grown women or cartoonishly threatening physical violence.

With the conception of the American as a cisgender, straight, white man, and usually a hypermasculine John Wayne type to boot, anyone who was different could face brutality and harassment. As a result of the Cold War, the fear of Communists living among us touched off a reaction that peaked with hearings by the House Un-American Activities Committee. The Civil Rights Movement had been organizing well before the 1960s in response to segregation and mob violence against African Americans. Emmett Till was murdered in Mississippi in 1955. The Stonewall Uprising in 1969 was preceded by years of persecution and protest. The federal government capitalized on paranoia internationally and at home to use surveillance as a weapon against groups identified as national threats. COINTELPRO, the FBI's secret program to infiltrate and discredit counterculture groups, began in 1956 and expanded in the 1960s.

It was against this backdrop that Nurmi began to create her character, which was in many ways the antithesis of these oppressive cultural forces. Nurmi unveiled a prototype of her subversive alter ego, Vampira, at the counterculture's carnival: dance teacher and choreographer Lester Horton's Bal Caribe Halloween bash in 1953. Poole describes Horton's ball as Nurmi's element: "The Bal Caribe represented the most outre gathering in 1950s Hollywood that brought together the city's gay elite, political radicals, and a hefty portion of campy glamour." The yearly event was notable both for the celebrities that it attracted and for the campy fashion that almost bordered on drag. Nurmi's Vampira-lite costume as a "female vampire" won the costume competition. It also won the attention of Hunt Stromberg Jr. at KABC. Her show *Dig Me Later, Vampira* premiered on KABC the following year, on April 30, 1954.

Nurmi's representation of Vampira—black hair, deathly pallor, sexy makeup, creepy low-cut black dress, and a horrifyingly outlandish figure (a shocking 36-17-36)—was a collage of several influences. One of her escapes when she was young was Milton Caniff's comic series *Terry and the Pirates*. Poole notes that Nurmi was especially fond of the independent character "The Dragon Lady," who was a "Chinese pirate queen" who alternated between being the villain and a kind of resistance fighter. Beyond her interest in independent and subversive representations of women, she gravitated to horror tropes like the vampire, the undead, and the witch to make people face the horrors of 1950s repression. For this, her strongest influence was Charles Addams's *New Yorker* cartoons about the family he called the Homebodies. The precursors to the TV show *The Addams Family*, Addams's stories about the Homebodies were much darker and took direct aim at American domestic conventions. Poole writes, "Addams suggested that the façade of the '50s housewife and the perfect suburban existence hid wishes for savage violence, a way to tear down the walls of containment in an apocalypse of rage." Nurmi liked Addams's challenge to conformity.

From her work as a model, Nurmi was highly aware of the innocent yet sexy image that the male gaze required of these objects of desire. She decided to give Vampira clear agency. She would subvert the male gaze by looking directly at the camera and by making bold costuming choices for a television show in the 1950s, including her belt, high heels, long fingernails, and demeanor. She may invite the viewer in, but Vampira is always in control. It is her show. And who, once they've heard it, can forget her shocking and orgasmic scream?

Dig Me Later, Vampira may have been a late-night horror movie host spot with skits, but it was extremely popular. It's difficult to know now what young people and their moms and dads were thinking when they watched it. We do know that they saw a complete subversion of what was represented on 1950s programs like *Leave It to Beaver*, *The Donna Reed Show*, or *Father Knows Best*. There was no visible husband on the show, and Vampira didn't do anything stereotypical housewives did. Poole says of her trademark opening scream: "She screamed instead of cleaning the house, washing the dishes, or falling in love with appliances. She screamed rebellion, a challenge to the high walls of containment and a symbolic middle finger raised toward the popular representation of the housewife." Her cocktail recipes were spooky and outlandish, her pet was a spider, and her bathtub was a cauldron.

Even her long makeup sessions and efforts to maintain her hourglass body proportions, in particular her tiny waist, were gothic statements on the rigorous labor women felt they needed to invest in their appearances for their husbands. Nurmi's intense body sculpting—which she achieved through deep fasting, intense heat and sweating, and the application of drying powders to her waist—mimicked the extreme dieting more mainstream women pursued. Even Samantha on *Bewitched* later in 1964 would tell her mother that she needed to break off a conversation to go make herself presentable for her husband's return home from work.

Unfortunately, there's very little footage left of Nurmi embodying Vampira. KABC didn't record the show. And sadly, the show didn't survive past a year, even with the national publicity Nurmi received from various appearances as Vampira and a spread on her in *Life* magazine in 1954. When her friend James Dean died in a car crash in 1955, rumors of her involvement in his death swirled, possibly adding to her difficulties with the TV station. Some fans of Dean developed the idea that she had cursed him using dark magic. Poole suggests that part of what may have fueled this interpretation was a comment Dean gave to a gossip columnist when he was romantically linked to Nurmi: "I don't date witches . . . and I dig dating cartoon characters even less." Here again, *witch* is used as a derogatory term for a woman who doesn't fit into a prescribed social position.

Nurmi passed away in 2008, and even though she hadn't portrayed Vampira in a long time, she hadn't lost her counterculture interests. She was embraced by the punk rock scene in the 1980s and 1990s. She collaborated with the band Satan's Cheerleaders. The Misfits' song "Vampira" was an homage to her character. Today, she's a cult horror figure remembered for her brief appearance in Ed Wood's 1957 B-movie *Plan 9 from Outer Space* and for Lisa Marie's portrayal of her in Tim Burton's 1994 movie *Ed Wood* about the life of the eccentric director. Perhaps, if Vampira hadn't tried to force her 1950s viewers to face their demons and had debuted in the looser 1960s, the show could have lasted longer. Nevertheless, she was a trailblazer in using the aesthetics of the occult to strike back at an oppressive culture, and it's not surprising that she was called a witch and accused of using dark magic when she did it.

BEWITCHED, THE LGBTQ+ ALLEGORY/ALLY

Bewitched was one of the most beloved television sitcoms of the 1960s, and it brought the occult into households across America. By today's standards, the show's messaging can be concerning. After all, it's about a wife with world-changing powers, whose mundane husband is constantly telling her to hide her true self and make herself powerless to help him. And for the most part, she wants to play the obedient housewife—though that often doesn't work, and sitcom hijinks ensue. But the show was quietly radical. After all, the women of Bewitched (Samantha, her daughter, and her mother) were all magical, making the female characters far more powerful than any of the male characters. And Samantha's mother, Endora, was an amazingly feminist character, as she did what she wanted, including taking many lovers, and she frequently prompted her daughter to live her life for herself and not anyone else (Darrin, we are looking at you).

But for many observers, Samantha's quest to balance her true self with her prescribed role is a queer allegory. Because of the lack of positive LGBTQ+ narratives, queer viewers often see themselves in explicitly heterosexual stories about self-acceptance and refusing to hide. (More recently, fifty years after Bewitched, some Disney fans read Elsa from *Frozen*, a princess with witch-like ice powers, as a queer character, casting her as a lesbian or even as an asexual woman in her quest to live outside of traditional society's rules.) Samantha is, after all, told that she has to stay in the closet. She has to hide her true self from her community, or else her family and reputation are at stake. In an interview with the *Advocate*, Elizabeth Montgomery, who played Samantha, said that she takes pride in the queer undertone of the show. She said, "Don't think that didn't enter our minds at the time. We talked about it on the set [. . .] that this was about people not being allowed to be what they really are. If you think about it, *Bewitched* is about repression in general and all the frustration and trouble it can cause. It was a neat message to get across to people at that time in a subtle way."

Following her time as the nose-twitching witch, Elizabeth Montgomery became a strong voice in advocating for the queer community. The cause became personal for her after her costar Dick Sargent (Darrin number two) came out of the closet in the 1990s. In fact, the two reunited in June 1992 as grand marshals at the Los Angeles Gay Pride Parade.

Laurie Cabot

During the Satanic Panic of the 1980s, groups like Jerry Falwell's Moral Majority insisted that Satan worshippers were at large and at work in America. But the real occult activity of the time was a lot less dramatic than worshipping the Christian idea of Satan. Following the new-age occultism and rise in Wicca during the experimentation of the 1960s and '70s, pockets of women quietly engaged with the occult, usually through covens or through generations of women teaching one another. One such woman was Laurie Cabot, a practicing but not public witch—still in the broom closet, so to speak—who found herself in Salem, Massachusetts, of all places. Cabot now owns a witchcraft shop called Enchanted on Salem's Pickering Wharf, but when she arrived in Salem in the late '60s, she wasn't practicing her witchcraft in public. At the time, Salem only had a small witch museum, and none of the witch-positive, Halloween fanfare that it boasts today. Eventually though, Cabot tired of keeping her lifestyle secret and opened Salem's first witchcraft storefront, called the Witch Shoppe.

Cabot made a name for herself in the field of witchcraft, culminating in the late '70s. In 1977, Massachusetts governor Michael Dukakis named her the "Official Witch of Salem" for her work with children with special needs. Two years later, Cabot and her coven were featured in *National Geographic*. Witchcraft, it seems, was back in vogue.

So in vogue, in fact, that Hollywood came calling. In 1986, a crew arrived at Salem's Crane Estate to film *The Witches of Eastwick*. The estate was to be the setting of Jack Nicholson's character's home. His character? Daryl Van Horne, the seductive new man in town who is quite literally Satan. (Or, as he describes himself in the movie, "just your average, horny little Devil.") Van Horne, in the film, awakens magic in three women—mostly through sex. Each woman gains enormous power (and quite a bit of freedom), but they are socially shunned because of their relationship with Van Horne. In short, the film depicts three witches who have sex with Satan, something the real witches of Salem took issue with.

Cabot led the charge against the film. She said *The Witches of Eastwick* relied on outdated and inflammatory views of witchcraft (after all, witches don't have sexual relationships with demons—they don't even believe in the Devil). Moreover, the setting of the Devil's home in the movie was problematic; in the film, it is said that he chooses the place because of its history, as it is where real witches were killed so many centuries ago. This didn't honor the real history of trauma in Salem, so Cabot and others protested.

In an interview with the *Washington Post* about *The Witches of Eastwick*, Cabot explained her anger: "Here are three women who have nothing better to do, because they are so frustrated sexually, than to get involved with witchcraft. They are not witches. If they are anything, they are weekend Satanists. They don't do one witchy thing in the whole film." For Cabot, the problem was with the way witchcraft was portrayed, something that witches have fought since this country was founded. As portrayed in the film—and in the historical trials—witchcraft was a religion that involved worshipping the Devil, specifically the Christian idea of Satan. Most people who identify as witches, however, do not have any association with the idea of the Devil, especially in this context.

Other religions are protected from misrepresentations—why, then, was witchcraft not afforded the same right? It didn't make sense to Cabot, and she decided to do something to remedy that.

And so the Witches' Civil Liberties League was born. Back then, it was called the Witches' League for Public Awareness. The group, led by Cabot, pushed for legislation that would protect witchcraft as a religion.

In an interview with *Faerie* magazine, Cabot did say that not all media portrayals of witches are bad ones. She's a fan of Samantha Stephens and of Angelina Jolie's Maleficent, explaining: "*Bewitched* showed magic being used every day, which is what witches do. [. . .] If [the television and film writers] would do research and know their history, they'd know how we really are."

With more positive media portrayals, witchcraft, and by extension the occult, was becoming more and more acceptable in the public eye. The occult, after all, often has very little to do with the Christian idea of hell or Satanism. In fact, most occult practice has very little to do with Christianity at all, as it stems from entirely different religious systems. And the religion from which her witchcraft stemmed, as Cabot explained in the *Washington Post* interview, was not scary or evil, nor was it about worshipping the Devil. Witchcraft, at its heart, is a nature religion, without a structure around a central deity. It is all about fair cultural representation. The first step toward acceptance and fair and equal treatment is understanding what the religion is actually about—and what it is not.

Elvira

While the Satanic Panic raged on in the United States and conservative parents everywhere were worried that the Devil was out to corrupt their children in Saturday morning cartoons and popular toys, one woman was able to walk through the '80s and '90s (and into the new millennium) unscathed. Her name? Elvira, Mistress of the Dark.

Elvira was the brainchild of actress Cassandra Peterson, who created her as a horror host for *Movie Macabre*, a show on Los Angeles's KHJ-TV. Prior to her iconic character, Peterson was a showgirl in Vegas (she started when she was only seventeen years old, and apparently went on exactly one date with Elvis). She also toured Italy for a while as a singer in a rock band and then worked for a time with the Groundlings. Of course, she is best known as the sexy goth queen Elvira.

As Elvira, she wears a long black dress, cut provocatively up her leg. Her cleavage is—well, there's a lot of it. Her nails are painted jet-black, to match her black bouffant hair. Her belt is decorated at the waist with a dagger.

Is she a witch? Is she a vampire? Whoever she is, she's clearly dangerous, not the virtuous mother that the 1980s seemed to want to extol. At least, it seems like she's exactly the type of woman who would be demonized by the conservative voices of the Satanic Panic.

But Elvira is fascinating in the way she manages to sail right through the Satanic Panic unscathed. Like Vampira before her, Elvira pushes the boundaries of what is socially acceptable, offering the public a safe space to explore what is taboo. She's a woman who is comfortable with her own sexuality. She's all about sex positivity, and she knows how to take care of herself around men who want to control her. Through her example, she pushes forward what is acceptable for other women to do, too. It's a kind of subversive feminist pop-culture activism.

In 1988, Elvira starred in her own movie, *Elvira: Mistress of the Dark*, which functions as a kind of microcosm of the Satanic Panic, especially as it relates to feminism and conservative family values. She's a career woman sexually harassed at work (the TV station's new owner wants to sleep with her) and she quits, mocking him in the process. She's in control of her own sexuality, but she's also rebelling against the narrative that single women are evil seductresses just waiting to sexually ruin a man at the first chance. It's a gothic *9 to 5*.

At the heart of the movie is the fictional town of Fallwell, Massachusetts, where she travels to claim her recently passed aunt's inheritance. A few notes here: Massachusetts is a significant place as the site of the Salem witch trials. But the name of the fictional town is also intriguing. The filmmakers have never commented on the choice, but it bears an uncanny resemblance to Jerry Falwell Sr., the televangelist who ran a megachurch in Virginia at the time. Along with Liberty University, his conservative Christian school, Falwell also led the Moral Majority, a political lobbying group that was behind some of the major political developments in the 1980s, including getting Ronald Reagan elected to the office of president. The Moral Majority, as a group, began in the '60s and '70s, as a direct reaction to the counterculture of the day. While the group didn't directly acknowledge its ties to fundamentalist Christian values, Falwell, like many of the group's supporters, promoted what would be considered extreme conservative ideals. The Moral Majority pushed politicians to vote against things like abortion access and gay rights, and to vote for things like prayer in school and anything that would support so-called traditional gender roles for men and women. The group saw their mission clearly: to clean up the moral corruption that threatened the nation and to reinstate good, clean (read: white, straight, cisgender, patriarchal) values.

Fallwell, the town in Elvira's film, is presented as the kind of American small town where teenage girls are berated by their grandmothers for wearing makeup and the local movie theater can only show G-rated movies. Elvira is only in town for a few minutes before she's accused of being the Antichrist. In a funny moment, just seconds after she's called the Devil, three handsome and wholesome-looking teenage boys literally trip over themselves to help her. This seems to be the fear of all the people in the town: a satanic temptress will take the "virtue" from their children. The movie, in this way, makes light of the entire Satanic Panic. One panicked townsperson even worries that a woman like Elvira in town means sex education in the schools and "passing out condoms to kindergarteners."

The townspeople, led by Chastity Pariah (the mockery isn't always subtle), are so concerned that Elvira will be a corrupting influence that they miss the true danger in town: Vincent, who wants to raise the "master of the dark" through actual occult means. There's an actual tar-and-feathering moment in the film, meant to publicly humiliate Elvira, followed by the climax, in which the town builds a pyre to burn the witch at the stake. The burning scene is like campy Shirley Jackson, as blonde Girl Scouts roast marshmallows over Elvira's pyre. This is Elvira's movie, though, and she is triumphant, managing to turn most of the townspeople to her side.

The tone of the film is pure camp, but that helps too. Comedy, like horror, pushes the boundaries of what is acceptable. It also helps acclimate the audience to feminist ideals without bringing about condemnation. In fact, Elvira is mimicking Vampira, who also used comedy to mock conservative values in a way that made her critique more palatable.

The similarities between Elvira and Vampira weren't lost on Maila Nurmi. She publicly claimed that Peterson plagiarized her look, but Peterson and the television station refuted those claims. And even though they both don black costumes and revel in the macabre, Elvira is entirely unique. Elvira is all Vegas glitter goth witch, with more than a touch of camp, but she's also restructuring the patriarchal narrative of the 1980s. She's a feminist icon in occult drag, the perfect woman to mark an end to the Satanic Panic (at least in pop culture) and lay the path for the witches that would emerge into power in the 1990s. And Peterson's still restructuring the narrative, even in the new millennium. In 2021, she went public about her nineteen-year relationship with her female partner (and personal trainer) Teresa Wierson.

"Whatever curse you're born with, the scars or whatever, let them become a blessing, not a curse."

—Cassandra Peterson (Elvira)

Louise Huebner

Who exactly is Louise Huebner? She's the official witch of Los Angeles County, with a legal certificate to prove it. Born in 1930 in New York City, Huebner was steeped in magic from an early age, as she often claimed her occult knowledge was passed along from her grandmother, who was an astrologer. She claimed six generations of witchy women in her lineage, stemming from her "Yugoslav-Greek ancestry." In an interview with *Vice*, Huebner claimed that she has possessed psychic powers since the age of two.

She looked the part of the sexy witch too; many publications commented on her long black hair. Her husband was Mentor Huebner, an artist who did storyboard work for film studios, working on films like *North by Northwest* and *Blade Runner*, to name only a few entries in his extensive catalogue.

Huebner made a career of her witchcraft, publishing love spells and offering tips for would-be witches on choosing the correct colored candles. She published ten books, including *Power through Witchcraft* and *Moon Magic*. She also released two spoken-word albums, including *Louise Huebner's Seduction through Witchcraft* in 1969.

The occult was the new way to express one's artistic sensibilities. It was slightly edgy, and it became fashionable to sell yourself as a witch—or at least someone with occult leanings. Case in point? Vincent Price, legendary horror actor and our perennial favorite, recorded a double album in 1969 called *Witchcraft & Magic: Adventures in Demonology.* It was macabre and at times overly theatrical, not unlike the man himself, but it was also a well-researched history of the occult.

Huebner's biggest stunt was an appearance at the Hollywood Bowl in July 1968. As her first duty as official witch, she invited the 11,000 people in the audience to join her in a sexual vitality spell. Employees handed out red candles (the color of lust), chalk, and garlic, as Huebner told the attendees to draw a circle around themselves, while they followed her in a chant. She also shared spells and potions with them. Whether or not the crowd felt anything following her spell, we may never know, but it did secure Huebner infamy as a "real" witch. She had been invited there to be part of a birthday party for the city, as well as to promote a series of concerts, the first of which was called "Folklore Day." Huebner was a local celebrity—and she was absolutely making the best of the fact that the occult was very much in fashion in the late 1960s.

As part of the Hollywood Bowl event, a county official gave Huebner a certificate naming her the Witch of Los Angeles. This was most likely a publicity stunt, as the event was being held as part of the county's parks and recreation department. Huebner, however, took her new title very seriously.

For the remainder of the year, she promoted various events around the city, though the Hollywood Bowl may have been her biggest group spell. As part of her "duties," Huebner was interviewed on national radio stations and over 350 television shows, both local and national. She lectured at Ivy League schools. She also said she did psychic readings and astrological consults for politicians and celebrities alike—and she frequently boasted that she got a lot of it right, including predicting JFK's assassination and the election of the first President Bush.

Huebner's reign as the "official witch" didn't come without controversy, though. Her beliefs were downright cringeworthy, and they didn't garner many fans. In a 1970 interview with the *Boston Globe*, Huebner said that not everyone could be a witch—she believed it was something a person inherited. More than that, she believed that a real witch is a woman by birth. "Any man who claims to be a witch," Huebner said, "or a warlock, has got to have homosexual tendencies. Witchcraft is closer to a woman's nature. The way a female expresses and experiences emotions. It's a very creative thing." While her sentiments may sound empowering for women, they are startlingly heteronormative and cisnormative, and she angered a lot of people in the budding occult community—particularly the newly formed Wiccan groups, because they felt excluded from her specific type of occult practice. She also has been outspoken about the fact that she is not a Wiccan, something that has earned her some scrutiny in witchcraft circles.

She also abused her title as "official" witch, at least to hear the county describe it. The Los Angeles County Counsel threatened to take away her title because she was "promoting herself as part of the official county government in selling her radio horoscopes and other charms." Apparently, her title was only meant for "fun and games for the parks and recreation department" and not in any sort of official capacity. Huebner responded that she'd "rescind all the good spells she's cast."

Selena Fox

The Satanists that Geraldo Rivera and the Christian mothers of America were so worried about during the Satanic Panic absolutely did not exist, at least not in the child-sacrificing, blood-bathing, Devil-worshipping kind of way that made the media. But women who engaged in the occult and pagan traditions absolutely did, only they were a bit quieter about it. The covens of the 1980s were much more engaged in environmental and civic activism than any kind of blood ritual; in fact, nature-based pagan religions do not pray to Satan at all (despite what the media said).

One woman working to change the incorrect perception in the media is Selena Fox through her work at the Circle Sanctuary.

Native to Virginia, Fox was born in 1949 and raised in a religious family with fundamentalist Southern Baptist values. Her spiritual education, however, started not within the church walls but outside, when she was communing with nature. Though these earliest experiences with the meditative power of nature were the initial stepping stones toward her pagan adulthood, she didn't have a real pagan education until she was a college student. She studied psychology at the College of William and Mary in Williamsburg, Virginia, but she also took classes in the classics, a love of hers. One moment, in particular, stoked her imagination—and led to her pagan spiritual awakening. As a college student, Fox was president of Eta Sigma Phi, the classics honor society, and as part of her duties, she planned a Rite of Spring, as an example of the kind of celebration that the ancient Romans may have enjoyed. There was flute and tambourine music, and everyone danced around outside as Fox acted as the priestess. In interviews, she has described this event as "ecstatic" and a "transformative experience." Soon after, she began to seek out groups of like-minded individuals, and it became her religion, though her pagan career would not begin until years later.

Fox gave up her corporate job in the late '70s to become a full-time witch. She is a minister at Circle Sanctuary, "a Nature Spirituality Church" and a resource center that she founded in 1974. In 1983, Circle Sanctuary Nature Preserve was established. Made a sacred land in 1988, the preserve is a 200-acre sanctuary in Wisconsin, which educates about wetland conservation while acting as a nature preserve. Since the sanctuary's inception, Fox has worked for Circle to be diverse, as she describes it in an online interview with Religioscope: "In our priesthood, we have a Mexican American Pagan who is of mixed Mexican and Spanish heritage. We also have a Native American Santee priestess who lives on the Lac-du-Flambeau reservation and she has married into [Anishinaabe] (Ojibwa) people. She also has some European ancestry. Early on, we started networking with people in Africa, and in Asia, in Latin America." That culture of acceptance moves beyond ethnicity and race too, as Fox and the other people of Circle work to make all comfortable in their community. For instance, Circle celebrates the national Transgender Day of Remembrance with a planned public ceremony as a part of their activism.

Over the decades, she has used her witchcraft as a form of activism, including working with the US Department of Veteran Affairs and other interfaith groups to get the pentagram included, as of

2007, on the list of emblems of belief that can be used to commemorate deceased veterans, including on burial sites and other official honors. Other social activism organized and promoted within Circle Sanctuary includes sponsoring Pride events and social justice workshops (recent topics included cultural appropriation).

Circle Sanctuary also works with volunteers and environmental scientists to bring about real environmental change. They are active in prairie restoration efforts (they work a lot with the nearby Oak Savannah Prairie), but they also work to promote local recycling efforts and participate in town meetings to bring preservation knowledge to discussions around land use proposals. In 1995, they also established one of the first green cemeteries in Wisconsin, where they offer natural burials of cremains and unembalmed bodies in biodegradable containers, like pine boxes or wicker caskets. As part of their continuing ecoactivism, Circle Sanctuary regularly participates in global efforts like International Earth Day and Climate Week and Global Climate Strike.

It makes sense: a religion that is based around nature will seek to protect nature, both so that it is preserved for future generations and so that it is marked as a sacred space for humans to experience connection with the earth.

Fox often speaks at conferences on her spiritual beliefs, and on the importance of activism in the occult community. She founded *Circle* magazine, which she also edits. Her other published works include *When Goddess Is God* and *Circle Guide to Pagan Groups: A Nature Spirituality Networking Sourcebook* in 1995 and 1979, respectively.

THE TEENAGE WITCH GROWS UP

HOW SABRINA CAME INTO HER POWER

Sabrina the Teenage Witch first appeared as part of the *Archie* comics universe in 1962, eventually getting her own series in the 1970s. In the 1990s, a television adaptation starring Melissa Joan Hart reintroduced her to pop culture. Like her comics counterpart, the 1990s iteration of Sabrina is presented as the average teenager. She's new at her high school, having trouble fitting in with the popular kids, and wondering how to get her crush to notice her. But on her sixteenth birthday, she learns she's a witch—by levitating in her sleep.

Of course, powers aside, Sabrina is still at her heart a "normal" teenage girl. She may be coming into her womanhood, but her power is still somewhat limited. In the opening credits, as an example, she is seen using magic to change outfits repeatedly, while checking herself out in the mirror. She uses her powers to get revenge on school bullies or to help her friends with relatively small problems.

The pop culture representation of witches in the 2010s and '20s has caught up with the activism that the real-life witches have always been involved in. Take Netflix's *The Chilling Adventures of Sabrina*. In this 2018 reimagining, Sabrina (played by the wonderfully talented Kiernan Shipka) is a powerful witch. She has to hide her powers from her mortal friends, of course, but even that doesn't last very long. This Sabrina is brave and gutsy—she isn't afraid to stand up to the Dark Lord or venture into hell to save her friends. But she also unapologetically enjoys her access to full and total power. She's "good," but she also enjoys the dark side.

Sabrina's mortal friends at Baxter High include Rosalind, a hereditary witch of color (played by Jaz Sinclair), and Theo Putnam (a trans character played by nonbinary actor Lachlan Watson). In one episode, Rosalind and Theo, determined to stop the harassment of female students on campus, form WICCA, or the Women's Intersectional Cultural and Creative Association. The club is a cheeky allusion to the history of witchcraft in America, honoring one of its long-standing traditions, but it also represents the witchy activism that is a cornerstone of the newest Sabrina.

Like her '90s counterpart, this Sabrina recognizes that a benefit of having power is the ability to help those who don't; it's part of her charm. But this Sabrina doesn't only use her power for good or to help others. She struggles with the idea of wielding power for power's sake, and the show explores the dangers inherent in that (especially as she eventually takes on the Dark Lord and essentially becomes the Queen of Hell). Once again, with great power comes great responsibility. Ultimate power often leads to a path full of darkness and danger.

Brandi Blackbear

A NEW WITCH PANIC AND CIVIL
LIBERTIES IN SCHOOLS

I n 1999, the American Civil Liberties Union in Colorado learned
that several middle school students had been harassed for being
witches. The incident, which took place at Panorama Middle
School in Colorado Springs, sounds like the beginnings of a new
witch panic. Apparently, one girl went to the school's library and
checked out a book on the Salem witch trials, which started her interest in the subject of witches in general. She shared her newfound
interest with her small group of friends, who responded enthusiastically; this unfortunately drew the taunts of other girls in the school,
who called them all witches. The girls then pretended to put spells
on their bullies. The bullying was so bad that some of the girls refused to return to school. The vice principal eventually got involved
and reportedly reprimanded the accused witches.

Unfortunately, this was not an isolated event. In 2000, the
Union Intermediate High School in Broken Arrow, Oklahoma, became embroiled in controversy when one student, fifteen-year-old
Brandi Blackbear, was suspended. The reason? She was accused of
witchcraft. More specifically, Blackbear was accused of making one
of her teachers ill. Blackbear was a typical student in a typical high
school. She liked to write scary stories in her notebooks (apparently
she was an avid Stephen King reader), and she often dressed in the

all-black goth style, popular post–*The Craft*. Blackbear also had a growing interest in Wicca.

That was enough for her school administration, who took her notebooks as "proof" of her witchcraft and told her she couldn't return to school for fifteen days. The American Civil Liberties Union intervened on Blackbear's behalf and took the case to the US District Court in Tulsa.

Brandi's father, Timothy Blackbear, spoke about his daughter's case, saying, "It's hard for me to believe that in the year 2000 I am walking into court to defend my daughter against charges of witchcraft brought by her own school." The case was eventually dropped, and in 2006, Lifetime aired *Not Like Everyone Else*, a made-for-TV movie about the court case, with actress Alia Shawkat playing Brandi Blackbear.

Witchcraft in schools was a concern for many parents and teachers across the country. In 1995, parents at the Charles Carroll Elementary School in Maryland took a second-grade reading list to a county education book council after they learned that the teacher planned to have the students read a book called *The Witch Goes to School*. The book is about a boy and girl who live next door to a girl who is a witch. One day, they are late to school, and the witch offers them a ride on her broom. They delight in her magic—but the witch won't help them magically do their homework. The book is about helping others, as well as acceptance and hard work. The parents, however, voted to ban the book from the list. One parent, who spoke with the *Baltimore Sun*, explained why she was against the book: "For people of faith, a lot of Christians and a lot of Jewish people, they don't want their children thinking of witches as good people, people they should be friends with." A witch being seen as a "good person" is apparently crossing a line for some.

American television evangelist Pat Robertson was one of the leaders in the cultural movement against witches. In a 1992 Iowa fundraising letter, he wrote, "The feminist agenda is not about equal rights for women. It is about a socialist, anti-family movement that encourages women to leave their husbands, kill their children, practice witchcraft, destroy capitalism and become lesbians." The letter was sent to Iowa voters in order to encourage them to vote against an Equal Rights Amendment that would protect women from discrimination. Robertson really had it out for witches and anything occult in the 1990s; he spoke out against *Sabrina, the Teenage Witch* (the version starring Melissa Joan Hart) as being "an example of insidious New Age thinking." Conservative talking heads also preached against the Harry Potter series and the games Dungeons and Dragons and Magic: The Gathering for promoting the use of witchcraft in the youth. It was the last gasps of the Satanic Panic, with grown men seeing the Devil's work in children's toys. But it was also deeply insidious, being used to promote the conversative idea that different was dangerous.

In a time when grown men were launching cultural witch hunts, and calling women who wanted equal rights witches and lesbians (to be clear, we don't see either of these as an insult—but Robertson did), it's notable that one of the landmark cases involved a fifteen-year-old child. Once again, the accusation of witchcraft amounts to a way for those who have power to chastise those who don't. In a way, it worked; Blackbear's parents eventually had to drop the suit. But the family's willingness to draw media attention to the injustice she suffered, and the ACLU's agreement to take the case, helped bring a broader concept of religious freedom into the public eye.

Krysta Venora

f we need more proof that the occult has entered the mainstream, we invite you to consider that Disney has entered the market. In 2021, Insight Editions released the Disney Villains tarot deck and guidebook, the only official tarot from the Mouse. They also introduced audiences to Krysta Venora, a practicing witch, on an episode (titled "Magic") in season two of *The World According to Jeff Goldblum*, streaming on Disney+.

In the episode, which looks into everything from show magicians and illusionists to the religious and spiritual aspect of the mystical, Goldblum visits a Los Angeles coven composed of self-proclaimed witches Kaitlyn Watsabaugh, Branché Foston, and Krysta Venora.

Goldblum calls himself "skeptical," though he acknowledges that these witches get something out of their practice. He sets up an ancestral altar with Venora. They channel Goldblum's ancestors. Goldblum cries: "I'll never be the same."

When Goldblum says that his "acting life caused me to seek maximum openness and interest in the unseen," Venora responds, "That's what magic has done for me. It lets you explore beyond the boundaries of what society says is possible and get to that place where you are open to endless possibility."

Venora is an Afro-Indigenous, trans, nonbinary, queer witch in

Los Angeles; they offer tarot readings, spiritual guidance, and rituals online under the name "Pink Opal Magic." Venora's background is in part Mormon, but they didn't always find acceptance in the strict religious community. Then their mother introduced them to Native American spirituality, another part of their heritage, and their world opened up.

In an interview with *Refinery29*, Venora explained their relationship to witchcraft: "[Witchcraft] gave me a sense of my personal power. . . . In this world, Black, indigenous, and queer people are told they have no power. So, to have something that gives me power and encourages me to use my voice and my will is invaluable." They describe their spiritual experience in the Mormon church as "profound," but say that they couldn't get past the church's rejection of their core being: "[The church] saw all these facets of my identity—black, indigenous, queer, survivor of childhood assault—as major sins. And I knew [that] was wrong." Wicca, which they were introduced to by a coworker, offered a route to spiritual fulfillment without the condemnation.

In 2021, during June's Pride month, the Salem Witch Museum sold a "Ride with Pride" T-shirt, a black T-shirt with a cartoon witch on a broom, silhouetted against a yellow moon. A rainbow, flanked by stars, erupts from her broom as she flies away. It's a great tee. It's also an interesting image, considering the witch's complicated history in Salem, a city that has had witchcraft tourism almost since the trials themselves. Not everyone has always been happy with the kitschy portrayal of the witch in the city, worrying that it downplays the death and destruction that resulted from the original persecution. But Salem as a whole seems to have embraced its nickname as Witch City, and the "Ride with Pride" shirts emphasized its commitment to be a place where witches of all kinds are welcome.

And, honestly, the convergence of queer activism and occult activism makes sense. Traditionally, in both history and folklore, witches and others who practiced (or were accused of practicing) the occult arts were those who didn't fit society's strict standards. This included women who weren't married, or weren't mothers, and men who didn't fit society's prescriptions for "male" behavior. Witches lived on the margins of society, sometimes desiring to leave society behind completely. Members of the queer community—those who identify as asexual, nonbinary, gay, lesbian, trans, and every other part of the spectrum—have, throughout history, been ridiculed, pushed to the edges, attacked and abused, and sometimes even killed. It's no wonder that the title "queer witch" has been reclaimed. It's a label that implies power, where once it carried fear.

Queer witch activism, it is important to note, has been around since the beginnings of the gay rights movement. Leo Martello, an openly gay man and a witch, was part of the era-defining Stonewall riots. Over the course of his life, Martello published books on witchcraft, fought for religious equality for Wiccan and pagan religions, and even sued the Catholic church for their participation in the persecution and deaths of witches in the past.

Religion is an important, and sometimes deeply loved, part of the human experience. The rituals, the prayers, and the communion with something greater than oneself are a critical part of many people's lives. It is devastating to be told that a person isn't welcome in their religious community because of who they are or who they choose to love. This leads many people to join occult and pagan religions instead. They are happy to embrace the rituals of a tradition that embraces them back. These alternative religious practices might explain why the occult world seems to be growing stronger each year. The world still seems uncertain. People are struggling to find work.

Politics have been like unstable fireworks shooting off in every direction. In 2020, a pandemic emerged, which raged and ravaged the world. The dumpster fire icon has been used too many times for comfort. Facing uncertainty, people have found solace in the ritual of the occult. If nothing else, it offers a community of encouraging and accepting people, and perhaps, a little bit of hope in a tarot reading. The occult sections of the internet offer a way for anyone to tap into a higher power, one that is more powerful than the problems of the world. And that is enticing, especially when other mainstream religions have told large groups that they are not welcome as they are. In this way, occult activism takes place as these practices position themselves directly in opposition to the Christian mainstream, a movement that often seeks to limit the rights of people who don't adhere to their tenets.

Rachel True

When *The Craft* entered the pop culture zeitgeist in the mid-'90s, it opened a world of occult power to hordes of teenage girls. The film was praised for its more realistic portrayal of witchcraft (as opposed to the fairy-tale pointed-nose witches of past pop culture), even though the god Manon that the coven worships is entirely a Hollywood invention.

As an actress, Rachel True entered horror and occult fandom with her portrayal of teen witch Rochelle in *The Craft*. Several of the people involved with the film had direct ties to the occult, which they brought to the set. True's costar Fairuza Balk brought her own witchy interests to the role (she owned a Wiccan store in Hollywood for a while). True's relationship with the occult, too, began long before filming began on the cult classic. She's quick to say that she's not "a pagan or a witch"—a claim she makes in the introduction to her *True Heart Intuitive Tarot*—but she is, as she describes herself, "a tad witchy." Her grandmother was rumored to possess the ability to predict the future, including when people were going to die. True is quick to point out that she cannot read anyone's future, but she could pick up on other people's energies. Even as a child, she was so good at doing this that she could almost read people's thoughts—something that didn't earn her many friends, especially as she was quick with the unwanted advice.

Even if True doesn't consider herself a witch in every sense of the word, she does find power in occult practices, like tarot cards, which led to her developing her own design of the popular deck. For True, the cards allow the reader to look into their inner self and see what is swirling around in the depths of their own subconscious. It's more Jungian psychology than Baba Yaga. The cards are about "developing and trusting your intuition," which for True brings empowerment. And that's better than any fortune that could be told.

In the guidebook that accompanies her deck, True relates bits about her own life and how the occult has interwoven with her personal history. When she first moved to Los Angeles to pursue acting, she writes about how tarot helped to ground and guide her even when she didn't fit in with all "the pale, white-skinned somnambulistic waifs who made up the bulk of Hollywood actresses." As she struggled to book jobs, she regularly meditated and pulled cards, keeping a notebook of her insights. Then, her chance came with *The Craft*, a movie role that attracted her in part due to occult elements.

This was her big break. Yet once again, she felt excluded from the industry she worked so hard to become a part of. Following filming, Sony set up a publicity trip to New York for an *Entertainment Tonight* interview. The main cast, Neve Campbell, Fairuza Balk, and Robin Tunney, were all invited, but Rachel True was not. True knew it was because she was the actress of color. If she were white, she'd be there.

Frustrated, True pulled a tarot card, the Wheel of Fortune. The message, she said, was: "This isn't about you specifically; you are simply a sentient being. This is about economics, race, and gender, which are all external things placed onto you by the society you live in." It was a moment of grounding that she desperately needed at that time. In the end, she was invited to publicity events, but only when her fellow performers fought for her to be included.

True still experiences a feeling of not fully fitting in, of being reduced to the "Black one." She writes, "Often black actors were relegated to civil servant roles, sassy prostitutes, or, my old standby, the black best friend. I'd been the token in any number of white-centric teen or twentysomething films and shows." Again, tarot worked to offer insight: "Tarot cards alert you when things are veering off-path and help silence the looping tape of negative self-talk by offering you an alternative way of thinking." In other words, if the outside world cannot accept, validate, or cheer you on, the occult community—and the tools it offers—can.

That is part of the allure of the occult, especially for people who don't feel accepted into mainstream society; it is something that can be meditative, offering much needed insight.

While the True Heart tarot deck is breathtakingly beautiful, the guidebook that accompanies the cards is one of the strengths. True approaches the explanation for each card with intellect and honesty, and each Major Arcana card includes a little bit of her autobiography, like peeks behind the curtain of someone who is a beautiful soul.

Witchcraft in the
Age of the Internet

Despite the manufactured fears of the Satanic Panic, the truth is that the 1990s still managed to be a time for the occult to blossom, as more women were engaging in occult activity in meaningful ways. Witchcraft and the occult were becoming more accessible to the average American teenager, largely thanks to one giant leap in technology: the World Wide Web. Prior to the widespread availability of the internet, occult practices were largely taught through familial tradition or within groups like covens—but now you could learn about witchcraft online at your home, school, or library. One major development in the spread of occult practices was the Witches' Voice (WitchVox), a website started in 1997 by Wren Walker and Fritz Jung, who had previously developed the website for the Witches League for Public Awareness, the civil action group started by Laurie Cabot. WitchVox aimed to be a place to collect positive press surrounding all things witchcraft, and where people could gather information about what it meant to be a witch. Walker wrote a lot for the site, with her own "Wren's Nest" column that passed along information on how to get started in witch-craft and included Wiccan frequently asked questions. WitchVox became a place for covens, practicing witches, occult shops, and other creatives to connect. At the time it closed in 2019, WitchVox had over 80,000 profiles of people eager to share their occult lives.

But before WitchVox, there was PODSnet, short for the Pagan and Occult Distribution Network. PODSnet started in the earliest days of the internet in the 1980s, reaching its peak activity in the early 1990s. PODSnet used an early form of internet communication that employed chat functions and message boards. One of the most useful as-pects was the "PODSnet Book of Shadows," a collection of all manner of occult information. This began a kind of oc-cult renaissance, coming to prominence alongside more occult books being published, like Silver RavenWolf's *Teen Witch: Wicca for a New Generation* in 1998. Other books and sites followed, including a teen section of WitchVox and the Children of Artemis, a witchcraft group that began in the UK in the mid-'90s but quickly grew to a large web presence around 1999. The Children of Artemis eventually published a magazine called *Witchcraft and Wicca*, which was specifically aimed at a younger audience. Occult re-sources were available in greater abundance than ever by the end of the twentieth century, and the occult commu-nity exploded in numbers.

The Witches of Social Media

FINDING CRAFT AND COMMUNITY ONLINE

People in the twenty-first-century occult community are having more conversations about what it means to be inclusive and ethical in their practices. In the twenty-first century women wear the mantle of "witch" proudly, and it is a source of power. But as we learned from Spider-Man, himself a kind of magic practitioner, with great power comes great responsibility.

The occult has become a lifestyle. Stores have begun to carry clothes best described as "witch aesthetic," and this fashion goes beyond the all-black apparel that was popularized immediately following the release of *The Craft*. Witches today can choose from a variety of fashionable options, from the cottagecore-esque "green witch" to "dark academia," which is a bit more buttoned-up (think tweed coats and turtleneck sweaters). And major retailers now carry occult beginner sets, so anyone who is interested in the occult can find a way to get started. Gone are the days of hiding. Women no longer have to rely on secretive internet boards or books handed down from older women. Today's woman interested in the occult may have gotten her start in the makeup megastore Sephora in 2018, where she spotted a "starter witch kit" containing tarot cards, rose quartz crystals, and white sage to burn in a cleansing ritual. Barnes and Noble now has an entire section devoted to tarot decks. Even Walmart and Amazon offer "sage smudge kits," with sage bundles ready to burn and feathers to use for all your cleansing ritual needs.

The occult is no longer hidden—it is widely accepted. This is a good thing, right?

Right?

People are happy for more accessibility, yes, but people are also upset. They are upset about mainstream culture co-opting the occult aesthetic. After all, witchcraft and similar practices are a religion for many, not a clothing style or a costume that someone can wear and take off as the whim hits them. This commercialization also brings up greater issues of cultural appropriation and environmental sustainability. Take those sage kits, for instance. Smudging is a long-held practice in many Native American and First Nations communities. It is an important religious and cultural ritual for groups like the Navajo, the Lakota, and the Cheyenne, just to name a few. So when white women run around their apartments, burning sage to clear the air after their latest bad breakup, it is cultural appropriation at its worst. Remember that kit at Sephora? Its sale upset so many people that Sephora ended up dropping the line. In fact, white sage is being sold at such a high rate today that it is being overharvested, causing a shortage. Now, those cultures that have used the herb for hundreds or thousands of years can no longer afford it.

Cultural appropriation is an important topic in today's occult communities, and one that is making headlines. The occult, at one time, meant a space that was free for experimentation (remember those California occult experiments in the first half of the twentieth century?), but now people are questioning how responsible it is to pick and choose your own personal occult path. For example, can a white woman call herself a bruja? Can she practice hoodoo, throwing around Florida water, just because she read about it on Pinterest?

The answer is a resounding no.

Women engaging in the occult is a wonderful thing. We have taken *witch*, a term that was used as an insult and an accusation of a crime and turned it into something that is synonymous with power. That is something that we do not want to lose.

However, in engaging with the occult and while bringing it mainstream, we must consider what it means when something that started as a counterculture movement becomes part of capitalism. We must consider all the implications of that shift from counterculture to cultural touchstone. And we must respect every person and group who is a part of that occult group.

In addition to becoming more vigilant about cultural theft, modern-day witches are following in Laurie Cabot's footsteps by taking a hard look at how Americans reckon with their witchcraft history. When looking at the celebration of witches in the US, it is impossible not to look at the queen of them all: Samantha Stephens of *Bewitched.* If you doubt her place as one of the most beloved witches in America, simply visit her bronze statue in the middle of Salem, Massachusetts. The statue itself seems to be a perfect example of the United States of America's conflicted relationship to the image of the witch and what happens when the image of the witch becomes relevant in the main cultural moment. When the statue was proposed in 2005, some residents of Salem protested the idea, telling NPR's *All Things Considered* that (in the words of NPR host Anthony Brooks) "a jaunty memorial to a TV sitcom witch abuses the memory of those who were persecuted in this city more than three centuries ago, when scores of people accused of witchcraft were rounded up and 19 of them hanged." People were murdered by the state, and it seemed in poor taste to erect a playful statue of a fictional witch so close to the site where actual people were hanged for witchcraft.

Others felt differently. After all, Salem had already reimagined its history and the figure of the witch, something that can be seen at nearly every tourist destination within the city, particularly around Halloween. However, while witch kitsch may be in, there's a real trauma that lies buried beneath.

Here's the good news: this increased scrutiny of cultural and historical insensitivity is also supporting a new kind of modern witch, who makes use of the popular witch aesthetic and the broad platform of the internet to teach others about the deeper roots of witchcraft. Bri Luna, who also goes by the name "the Hoodwitch," is the perfect example. She's social-media and internet savvy, but she comes from a hereditary line of witches and brujas (according to her website, Luna's "grandmother was a traditional Mexican spiritual healer"). She also has a rock-star-icon attitude, and she credits John Waters films and Marilyn Manson music as her witchy inspirations as much as anything else. Luna's career as a professional practitioner has been enormously successful and has led to work with companies like *Refinery29* and Almay. She also served as occult consultant on the 2020 film *The Craft: Legacy*, a continuation of the 1996 cult favorite. But more importantly, Luna speaks about how social media has led to more equality in the witch community. The occult tradition in the US, at least the visible and celebrated occult community, has been largely white ever since Salem. On her website, Luna speaks about the difficulty in breaking into a community dominated by white people and rituals with European roots: "Being a Black and Mexican woman, I always want to feel like I'm being represented, but that was missing. Classes and workshops that were available were primarily focused on Eurocentric forms of spirituality and Pagan traditions. Not so much African or Indigenous or Mexican."

Luna expresses one of the biggest draws for women to the occult. The default setting of mainstream American society is heteronormative, white patriarchy, informed by a Christian worldview with a vocal and aggressive conservative component. So what happens when a person's identity falls outside those narrow definitions? Logically, they search for community and connection elsewhere. As Luna demonstrates, the occult seems ready-made for women and people of color to connect not only with others who share similar values, but, maybe more importantly, with a community outside of the heteronormative white patriarchy. And so, we arrive at the idea of witchcraft and the occult as activism, as rebellion. After all, the title of witch, with all its complicated connotations, has been enthusiastically reclaimed.

Alice Sparkly Kat

POSTCOLONIAL ASTROLOGY AND
RESHAPING CULTURAL IDENTITIES

Astrology is inherently political. At least, that's the central premise of Alice Sparkly Kat's 2021 book *Postcolonial Astrology: Reading the Planets through Capital, Power, and Labor.*

Astrology (and the lens through which astrology allows us to view the world) is a personal subject for Sparkly Kat. Born in the Henan province in China, they immigrated to the United States as a young child. Life in small-town Iowa didn't offer everything Sparkly Kat needed. As a queer Asian American, they didn't see themselves in the culture. So, at eighteen, Sparkly Kat moved to New York because they needed to be surrounded by more people of color. Even in the vast melting pot of New York City, though, they still felt like a settler, as they describe in the introduction to their book: "I currently rent a room in Brooklyn as a non-Black gentrifier. I am an Asian settler in occupied Lenapehoking territory. I used to fantasize about going back to China, and I imagined I could cease to be a settler if I went back." Of course, that would never be a reality, as Sparkly Kat knew that gentrification and colonialism are present in China too, threatening Indigenous peoples. They also recognized that their own American upbringing would prohibit a true "belonging" to Chinese history and culture. It was a frustrating and alienating experience, leaving Sparkly Kat feeling far from their own history, culture, and ancestors.

They began studying astrology in 2014, following a particularly rough time in their life, which included a divorce. The queer astrology community in Brooklyn welcomed Sparkly Kat with open arms, but they noticed a bigger lack of people of color represented in astrology as a whole. There were few books from the perspective of a person of color.

Astrology was almost wholly filtered through a Western lens. As Sparkly Kat explains in their book, "the history of astrology developed out of white supremacy and patriarchy." As an example, we gender the planets, when we talk about Venus and Mars (largely due to how history has spoken about their counterparts in the Roman pantheon of gods and goddesses). Not only that, but the consistent use of Roman terms for the stars and other astrological terms affirms a Western hegemony. This perhaps explains why the occult—astrology included—has been embraced by American conservatives like the Reagan administration, as well as by (in the extreme) full-blown fascist groups like the Nazis. That doesn't mean, however, that astrology in and of itself is a flawed system. It is all in how we talk about it.

Astrology can be used to break social norms. Sparkly Kat used their background in writing fanfiction to begin to reimagine how to talk about astrology. In fanfiction, they were used to creating new stories with characters that don't belong to them; as they explain it, "it is a community that contests the authority of authorship." Astrology belongs to the community—the fans—and they control the narrative and language of the system. As Sparkly Kat wrote in their book, "My mission with astrology is this: to take back the language of the cosmos from capitalism and supremacy and to use it for the creation of communities of care." They credit astrology for giving them a language to help communicate and heal within a white, patriarchal society. It didn't heal those wounds inflicted, but it did give them new tools in their toolbox. If the West is a construct, if the concept of whiteness is a story that we keep telling in order to reinforce it, then we can choose different ways of telling stories while beginning to heal the trauma of those original stories that privilege the West and whiteness. As Sparkly Kat writes: "Good astrology acknowledges and resists capital, power, and labor. Good astrology shrinks the West. There is no one way to practice astrology."

Today, Sparkly Kat is still in Brooklyn, working as an astrologer, where they give personal consultations, office-based group training sessions (think coworker-bonding activities and the like), events, classes, and workshops. They have spoken on postcolonialism in museums (discussing astrology and art), including MOMA, the Brooklyn Museum, the Philadelphia Museum of Art, and the Hauser and Wirth Gallery. Sparkly Kat's books include *Astrology and Storytelling* and *Planetary Alignment for Mental Bliss* (a workbook combined with a coloring book), both available on Sparkly Kat's website.

In a way, it is fitting that we end this book with a person like Alice Sparkly Kat. We began with Salem, when even the rumor of witchcraft could mean a death sentence. It was a time when conforming to society was a means of survival. But so much has changed. Now, while the public's feeling toward the occult may change, swinging from acceptance to criticism, the arc is bending toward inclusivity.

"Good astrology
acknowledges and resists
capital, power, and labor.
Good astrology shrinks the
West. There is no one way to
practice astrology."

—Alice Sparkly Kat

mbracing the occult can be a means to fame, fortune, or political influence, but it is so much more than that. It is a religion; it's also activism. But at its best, it's about finding personal power within oneself and then using that power to affect change in societal structures, working toward a more ethical and inclusive narrative. The occult is inherently nonbinary. It is open to all possibilities. Through the occult, individuals can create new spaces for themselves, while simultaneously dismantling the mainstream stereotypes for how people should identify and behave.

Performers like Vampira and Elvira offered their versions of gothic femininity as a way of challenging the status quo and changing how people viewed the role of women within society. Today, we are seeing even more of that play out in the public space. Krysta Venora and Alice Sparkly Kat are embracing different aspects of the occult, but at the same time, they are using the language and tools of the occult to change the conversations that people are having about ideas like gender, history, and inclusivity. This change is occurring both within the occult community (which, in the past, has had a tendency to use limiting language centered on the female body, in particular the white female body) and the greater outside world, as a fight for equality affects us all.

CONCLUSION

The occult, as we've seen, has offered a ready-made community for women who couldn't fit into patriarchal, Eurocentric society—or who didn't want to, because they didn't like the role given to them. However, for centuries, the word *witch* has been used as an insult, casting these "misfits"—those who are poor, single, widowed, rebellious, ambitious, or outspoken—as dangerous or even demonic. The negative stereotype of a woman steeped in the occult has been baked into our very language and is a long-standing trope of our folklore and popular culture.

In fairy tales and Disney movies, the occult woman (often labeled *witch*, even if that wasn't accurate) was the villain, most likely old and haggard, the one waiting to wreck someone's "happily ever after." She lured children to her oven with a house made of gingerbread and candy. She pricked the fingers of unsuspecting girls with her enchanted spindle, causing them to fall asleep and almost miss their future happiness as the wife of Prince Charming. Her weapons were found in the home, but her target was traditional domesticity. The witch might have something bubbling over her fire, but it wasn't dinner. It could be a healing brew, or it could be a poisonous spell. It could even be an ointment to help her magically fly, made from babies she kidnapped and murdered. She might have a broom simply to keep a clean house, but she *could* be using it to fly through the night. And, depending on who was telling the tale and when they were telling it, she might be flying to visit her demon lover or to steal a man's penis for nefarious purposes (remember the *Malleus Maleficarum?*).

But even if the occult woman was cast as an outsider, there's still an undeniable power and complexity in the witchy woman. Maleficent and the Evil Queen always had more power and agency than Sleeping Beauty and Snow White. Besides, everyone knows that Maleficent was so much cooler than Sleeping Beauty (we'd much rather play with dragons than marry the prince any day).

The witch was representative of the subversion of everything society told her she *should* be: the good wife, the loving mother, the keeper of the home. If society told her she was unfit, she packed her bags and moved to the outskirts of town and closer to nature, where she didn't have to be a part of society's rules. She had no husband, so she kept control of her own life. She had no children, so she could care for herself and others. In real life, early "witches," or local healers, while presented in fairy tales as overwhelmingly evil, were often approached for their wisdom and remedies. They could be caretakers to communities, rather than a single family.

Indeed, society often used witchcraft as a label for someone who didn't, or couldn't for reasons out of their control, conform to communal hierarchies and rules. If women stood up for themselves, or were in the way, or didn't conform, or were a little too powerful, or a little too strange, an accusation of witchcraft could solve the problem. When these social conflicts were solved through accusations of demonic behavior and witchcraft, the solutions sowed terror throughout intensely religious and patriarchal communities. And the solutions were cruel and violent. This has happened multiple times: first in Salem, then in the Satanic Panic, and even today, where we see hints of it in QAnon conspiracy theories. Still, occult traditions have always survived these periods of backlash, and often emerged stronger than ever. Perhaps this is because of what the occult represents.

The occult has always been about embracing a powerful idea of self—discovering that "yes, I am exactly who I need to be." This book's journey through occult history has been a long and winding one. We've gone from the Salem witch trials through the female mediums of Spiritualism in the nineteenth century to women using the occult as activism and to transform the language of patriarchal religion during second-wave feminism in the mid-twentieth century. Along the way, and up to our current moment, while women were designing these larger resistance movements, they also were experimenting with astrology, fortune-telling, spells, and other elements of the occult. That experimentation has only grown exponentially as occult communities have embraced the internet, especially social media. Throughout the decades, the occult was, at times, accepted with open arms, but we also saw periods of backlash, when witches everywhere had to go back in the broom closet. One thing we've noticed over the centuries is that the arc of the occult is bending toward inclusivity. Today, conversations about keeping the occult world more ethical and inclusive are happening more than ever. And because so many in the occult community are social activists, we hope that these conversations are moving into the mainstream world, too.

SELECTED BIBLIOGRAPHY

FOR A COMPLETE LIST OF REFERENCES CONSULTED,
VISIT QUIRKBOOKS.COM/TOILANDTROUBLE.

Adler, Margot. *Drawing Down the Moon: Witches, Druids, Goddess-Worshippers, and Other Pagans in America Today*. Originally published in 1979. Boston: Beacon Press, 1986.

Baer, Hans A. *The Black Spiritual Movement: A Religious Response to Racism*. 2nd ed. Knoxville: University of Tennessee Press, 2001.

Baker, Emerson W. *A Storm of Witchcraft: The Salem Witch Trials and the American Experience*. Oxford: Oxford University Press, 2016.

Barstow, Anne Llewellyn. *Witchcraze: A New History of the European Witch Hunts*. San Francisco: Pandora, 1994.

Beck, Richard. *We Believe the Children: A Moral Panic in the 1980s*. New York: PublicAffairs, 2015.

Berger, Helen A., and Douglas Ezzy. *Teenage Witches: Magical Youth and the Search for Self*. New Brunswick, NJ: Rutgers University Press, 2007.

Blum, Deborah. *Ghost Hunters: William James and the Search for Scientific Proof of Life After Death*. New York: Penguin, 2006.

Braude, Ann. *Radical Spirits: Spiritualism and Women's Rights in Nineteenth-Century America*. 2nd ed. Bloomington: Indiana University Press, 2001.

Brownmiller, Susan. *In Our Time: A Memoir of a Revolution*. New York: Dial Press, 1999.

Cep, Casey. "Why Did So Many Victorians Try to Speak with the Dead?" *New Yorker*, May 24, 2021.

Clifton, Chas S. *Her Hidden Children: The Rise of Wicca and Paganism in America*. Lanham, MD: AltaMira Press, 2006.

Demos, John. *The Enemy Within: A Short History of Witch-Hunting*. New York: Penguin, 2008.

Dore, Mary, dir. *She's Beautiful When She's Angry*. Originally released in 2014. Chicago: Music Box Films, 2016.

Echols, Alice. *Daring to Be Bad: Radical Feminism in America, 1967–1975*. 30th anniversary edition. Minneapolis: University of Minnesota Press, 2019.

Federici, Silvia. *Caliban and the Witch: Women, the Body, and Primitive Accumulation*. New York: Autonomedia, 2004.

Forbes, Erin E. "Do Black Ghosts Matter?: Harriet Jacobs' Spiritualism." *ESQ: A Journal of Nineteenth-Century American Literature and Culture* 62, no. 3 (2016): 443–79.

Gardner, Gerald. *Witchcraft Today*. Originally published in 1954. Ancient Crafts Publishing, 2020. Kindle.

Goldsmith, Barbara. *Other Powers: The Age of Suffrage, Spiritualism, and the Scandalous Victoria Woodhull*. New York: A. A. Knopf, 1998.

Grossman, Pam. *Waking the Witch: Reflections on Women, Magic, and Power*. New York: Gallery Books, 2019.

Horowitz, Mitch. *Occult America: White House Seances, Ouija Circles, Masons, and the Secret Mystic History of Our Nation*. New York: Bantam Books Trade Paperbacks, 2010.

Jaher, David. *The Witch of Lime Street: Séance, Seduction, and Houdini in the Spirit World*. New York: Crown, 2016.

Janisse, Kier-La, and Paul Corupe, eds. *Satanic Panic: Pop-Cultural Paranoia in the 1980s*. Godalming, UK: Fab Press, 2016.

Kalush, William, and Larry Sloman. *The Secret Life of Houdini: The Making of America's First Superhero*. New York: Atria Books, 2007.

Karlsen, Carol F. *The Devil in the Shape of a Woman: Witchcraft in Colonial New England*. New York: W. W. Norton, 1998.

Kasson, John F. *Houdini, Tarzan, and the Perfect Man: The White Male Body and the Challenge of Modernity in America*. New York: Hill and Wang, 2001.

Kramer, Heinrich, and James Sprenger. *Malleus Maleficarum (The Witch Hammer)*. First German edition 1487. Translated by Montague Summers, 1928. Updated translation 1948. Pantianos Classics, 2016.

Mackenberg, Rose. *Houdini's "Girl Detective": The Real-Life Ghost-Busting Adventures of Rose Mackenberg*. Compiled and edited by Tony Wolf. CreateSpace, 2016.

McGarry, Molly. *Ghosts of Futures Past: Spiritualism and the Cultural Politics of Nineteenth-Century America*. Berkeley: University of California Press, 2008.

Morgan, Robin. *Sisterhood Is Powerful: An Anthology of Writings from the Women's Liberation Movement*. New York: Random House, 1970.

Morton, Lisa. *Calling the Spirits: A History of Seances*. London: Reaktion Books, 2020. Kindle.

Poole, W. Scott. *Vampira: Dark Goddess of Horror*. Berkeley: Soft Skull, 2014. Kindle.

Quigley, Joan. *What Does Joan Say?* New York: Pinnacle, 1990.

Regan, Donald T. *For the Record: From Wall Street to Washington*. New York: Harcourt, 1988.

Roach, Mary. *Spook: Science Tackles the Afterlife*. New York: W. W. Norton, 2006.

Schiff, Stacy. *The Witches: Suspicion, Betrayal, and Hysteria in 1692 Salem*. New York: Back Bay Books, 2016.

Starhawk. *The Spiral Dance: A Rebirth of the Ancient Religion of the Great Goddess*. 20th anniversary edition. New York: Harper One, 1999.

Tanner, Amy E. *Studies in Spiritism*. New York: D. Appleton and Company, 1910.

Valiente, Doreen. *The Rebirth of Witchcraft*. Originally published in 1989. London: Robert Hale, 2017. Kindle.

Weisberg, Barbara. *Talking to the Dead: Kate and Maggie Fox and the Rise of Spiritualism*. New York: Harper Collins, 2005.

Young, Jeremy C. "Empowering Passivity: Women Spiritualists, Houdini, and the 1926 Fortune Telling Hearing." *Journal of Social History* 48, no. 2 (2014): 341–62.

INDEX

174–82, 218–22, 223–25. *See also* embracing the occult; occult; paranormal investigation; professional occultists

Witches' Civil Liberties League, 236

Witches' League for Public Awareness, 216

Witches of Eastwick, The (1986), 235

Witches' Voice (WitchVox), 260–61

Witch Goes to School, The (Bridwell), 251

WitchTok, 108–9

Wizard of Oz, The (1939), 86–87

women: Christ on bonds among, 61; disenfranchisement and exclusion of, 20–21, 67, 95, 113, 167; and Dungeons and Dragons, 191; employment of, 101–2; "good" versus "bad," 29–30; and opposition to occult, 211, 215; and paranormal investigation, 193, 203, 206; relationship with occult, 10, 12–13, 14–15, 71–72, 214–15; and risk of witchcraft accusation, 183–85; and sexual repression in Victorian England, 40; societal expectations for, 13, 29–30, 72, 116; and Society of Universal Friends, 24–25; Spiritualism and, 58, 70–71, 116, 192–93, 197; studies

on intelligence of, 197; trans women, 11, 62; vulnerability of marginalized, 178–79; witchcraft and, 16. *See also* gender

Women's International Terrorist Conspiracy from Hell (WITCH), 97–100

Wonderful Wizard of Oz, The (Baum), 86

Woodhull, Victoria, 13, 72, 73–76, 113

X-Files, 135, 202–3

Yeats, William Butler, 37, 94

Young, Jeremy C., 91–92

YouTube, 108

zap actions, 97

ACKNOWLEDGMENTS

If only writing a book were as easy as twitching our noses . . .

If only.

Writing a book takes a community. And we are thankful to our publishing community for helping us bring this little occult book to life. First, Melanie and Lisa would like to thank Quirk Books, especially our fantastic editors, Jess Zimmerman and Rebecca Gyllenhaal. Good editors are wizards, who can take a manuscript of words and ideas and help to mold it into the right structure for a book. It is nothing short of magic, and we are grateful. We'd also like to thank all the librarians who helped us in our research journey—the world is better because we have libraries.

We'd also like to express our heartfelt gratitude to Ann Leslie Tuttle, who is simply the best agent these two writers could have.

Thank you, too, to Caitlin Keegan for the incredible artwork. You have made our book a work of art. And we'd also like to thank the readers of *Monster, She Wrote*, and those who listen to us on the *Monster, She Wrote* and *Know Fear* podcasts; this community of horror readers has been so supportive of us. And to Matt Saye—thanks for going on this podcast journey with us. For that, we are truly grateful.

Lisa has to thank the best writing (and podcasting) partner around, Melanie Anderson. Every book we do together is a dream come true (and a fun journey). I'm appreciative of my writing community for keeping me on track and giving me much needed guidance (and more than a few laughs), especially Larissa Zageris, Mo Moshaty, Melody Cooper, Kelly Krause, and Kait Nolan. And to the writers who have taken the time to talk craft with me: special thanks to Andy Davidson, Grady Hendrix, and Glen Mazzara. I'm also forever grateful for my circle of friends (who offer constant support), especially Emily Jones, Kelly Lundquist, Natalie Davis, and Jenny Hyest—thank you for only being a text or a phone call away. As always, I wouldn't be here without my family, including my mom and dad and sister, Ginger, as well as my niece and nephews. (To Lily: I'm writing spooky stories for you!) The most heartfelt thanks go to Robbie, Leo, and Eli. Thank you for always loving me. My boys, everything I do is for you.

Melanie must thank Lisa Kröger for always making the material better and the process a joy, whether we are writing books or creating podcast episodes. A shout-out must go to Shari Holt for helping me overcome pandemic-related research obstacles. I'm also grateful to my friends for their support, especially when things were locking down in 2020 and we needed to rely on Skype and Zoom to stay connected. Writing is a part of what I do as a professor, alongside classroom teaching and service, and I'm thankful I work with fantastic and supportive colleagues in the Division of Languages and Literature at Delta State University. As always, the utmost gratitude goes to my family, especially my parents, for their support. And thank you to Bobbie, one of the best of man's best friends, who has been napping while I write and making me take breaks for walks for over a decade.

ABOUT THE AUTHORS

LISA KRÖGER is the coauthor of *Monster, She Wrote*, as well as the cohost of the *Know Fear* and *Monster, She Wrote* podcasts. She's won the Bram Stoker Award and the Locus Award. Lisa's contributed fiction and nonfiction to *Lost Highways: Dark Fictions from the Road*, *EcoGothic*, *The Encyclopedia of the Vampire*, and *Horror Literature through History*. Her essay collections include *The Ghostly and the Ghosted in Film and Literature: Spectral Identities* and *Shirley Jackson: Influences and Confluences*. Lisa is an active member of the Horror Writer's Association and a core member of the NYX Horror Collective, a group focused on women-created genre content for film, television, and new media.

MELANIE R. ANDERSON is an assistant professor of English at Delta State University in Cleveland, Mississippi. She is the coauthor of *Monster, She Wrote* and the cohost of the *Know Fear* and the *Monster, She Wrote* podcasts. Her book *Spectrality in the Novels of Toni Morrison* (University of Tennessee Press, 2013) was a winner of the 2014 South Central MLA Book Prize. She has coedited three essay collections: *The Ghostly and the Ghosted in Literature and Film: Spectral Identities*, *Shirley Jackson, Influences and Confluences*, and *Shirley Jackson and Domesticity: Beyond the Haunted House*.